BRAND HARMONY

BRAND HARMONY

Achieving Dynamic Results
by Orchestrating Your
Customer's Total
Experience

STEVE YASTROW

Tom Peters Company Press
An imprint of SelectBooks, Inc.

This edition published by SelectBooks, Inc.
For information address
SelectBooks, Inc., New York, New York 10003

First Paperback Edition

ISBN 978-1-59079-199-8

The Library of Congress has cataloged the hardbound edition published
in 2003 by SelectBooks, Inc. as follows:

Library of Congress Cataloging-in-Publication Data

Yastrow, Steve, 1959–

Brand Harmony: achieving dynamic results by orchestrating your
customer's total experience / Steve Yastrow.—1st ed.

p. cm.

ISBN 1-59079-053-7

1. Brand name products. 2. Business names. 3. Marketing. I. Title.
HD69.B7Y47 2003
658.8'27--dc21

2003004305

Manufactured in the United States of America

10 9 8

*"There is nothing either good or bad
but thinking makes it so."*
—Hamlet, Act II, Scene 2

The Tom Peters Company Press
An Imprint of Select Books

Since the initial publication of *In Search of Excellence* in 1982, Tom Peters has been "inventing the new world of work," by calling attention to the ideas and insights that will move the business world ahead into the future.

Now, Tom Peters Company has joined forces with Select Books to create The Tom Peters Company Press, an imprint dedicated to showcasing the business ideas that will make a difference in the future. The Tom Peters Company Press reinforces Tom's tradition of bringing the best in new business thinking to the millions of people who have purchased Tom's books and heard him speak in person.

Brand Harmony is the first book in this series, with more titles planned to follow. To learn more about The Tom Peters Company Press, contact Kenzi Sugihara at 212-206-1997.

Contents

Acknowledgements

This book is dedicated to my family, who make everything possible:
My wife – Arna
My kids – Nurit, Levi & Noah
My parents – Sybil & Shelby
My siblings – Sara & Phil

I now understand the sincerity of the statement, "Nobody writes a book alone," with which many authors open their acknowledgements. An author can work in isolation no more than a painter can work without light; the feedback, ideas and insights of others have illuminated my ideas on marketing as I have developed *Brand Harmony*. I regret that the space here only allows me to credit some of those with direct input on this book; my views have been shaped by interactions with many other people who can't be mentioned here. Thanks to all of you.

First, I want to acknowledge my wife, Arna. Lucky me, I married a former editor with perfect pitch for language and written communication.

Many thanks to...

- My father, Shelby Yastrow, and my father-in-law, Ben Sosewitz, who act as my personal board of directors and always asked the tough questions. Their wisdom and insights have helped me see my subject matter more clearly.
- My writing group and close friends, Karyn Kedar and David Gottlieb. Their talent set a high bar for me to aim at during our Friday morning sessions at Borders.

- Julie Anixter, Erik Hansen, Boyd Clarke, Tom Peters, Ron Crossland, Geoff Thatcher and other friends at tompeterscompany! who have helped me immeasurably. Consulting to Tom Peters during a time period in which he produced three books and conceived a new seminar gave me an invaluable opportunity to see a master at work, and I will use that lesson forever.
- Kenzi Sugihara of Select Books deserves a special thank you for taking the plunge and giving me the freedom to express myself. His advice, guidance and mentoring through this process have been invaluable. Thanks also to the rest of the Select Books crew who helped me: Maryglenn McCombs, Todd Barmann, Kenichi Sugihara, Julie Schwartzman and Kathleen Isaksen. Thanks also to Gail Kump of Midpoint Trade Books for her insights, recommendations and support.
- Jim Harris, a brilliant thinker who has inspired my ideas about marketing in ways I could never measure.
- Thomas Schacht of Midt Marketing, for introducing Brand Harmony to Denmark.
- Rachel and Chuck Rosenberg, my close friends and musical collaborators, for the brainstorming session that created the subtitle for this book.
- A number of friends participated in critical reads of the manuscript, providing valuable advice and insights: Sam Henry, Adam Blonsky, Brian Kovach, Diana Lackner, Tami Warshawsky, Amanda Kinslow and my brother, Phil Yastrow.
- Neal Kusnetz, who, during a conversation about Brand Harmony somewhere on 6th avenue and sometime after midnight, had the insight, "A brand is a thought."
- Sara and Bob Silver at Silverware and Joe Murphy of Joe Design for their help with brandharmony.com and our Internet marketing activities.

And, of course, thanks to most of the big ad agencies I've ever worked with, for showing me what's wrong with mass marketing. Guess what: The emperor really does have no clothes!

How to Use This Book

How many people does it take to create Brand Harmony?

This book can have a powerful impact on the performance of your organization, whether you are an entrepreneurial start-up, a Fortune 500 company or anything in between.

Go ahead! Read it! I trust it will give you insights that you can start applying immediately to your business, whatever it is.

But don't stop there. Enlist the involvement of your colleagues and co-workers. One of the bedrock principles of Brand Harmony is that your customers are paying attention to everything your organization does, which means that Brand Harmony succeeds when people throughout an organization cooperate in its creation.

As you start reading this book, even from the opening story at the beginning of chapter 1, start thinking of the people in your organization whose involvement will make Brand Harmony work for you. Who in your organization has a major effect on customer experiences? Who really "gets it," with a clear picture of what your company does well and not so well? Who has the influence to credibly spread the word about Brand Harmony throughout the company? (Don't just look at the "assigned leaders," i.e., senior people. Look for those with "earned leadership," whose influence comes purely from their abilities, insights and experience.)

As soon as possible, get those people involved with Brand Harmony. Here are some ideas:

Go to www.brandharmony.com/invite where you'll be able to send these people information about Brand Harmony and how it can help your organization.

Form a Brand Harmony reading group with these colleagues where you can brainstorm the ideas in the book and work through the implementation steps. See www.brandharmony.com/reading group for ideas and information. (Also, see the appendix "What to do when you finish reading this book" for more ideas.)

As your core group gains momentum, start to broaden your circle, inviting more people into the process. Your goal is to create a "grass roots Brand Harmony movement" in your organization that comes to be considered as a legitimate strategic process.

And, the most important piece of advice as you enter the world of Brand Harmony: **Stay With It.** Creating Brand Harmony isn't a task you can check off a list. It's a way of doing business that starts today and continues forever. Your customers are listening; now is the time to start paying attention to what they're hearing.

1

The Parable of the Concert

How Was Your Experience?

Imagine yourself attending a symphony orchestra concert.

The players are ready on the stage. The conductor lowers his baton to start the piece. But almost as soon as the concert begins, you notice that you are distracted by noises coming from different places in the auditorium. You look to your left and see a workman climbing a ladder, who then starts to use loud power tools to repair a hole in the auditorium wall. You look to the stage, expecting to see the conductor jump into a fit of rage because his concert has been interrupted, but the conductor is still conducting and the players are still playing. You realize that he and the musicians haven't heard the workman's disruptions.

Suddenly you are distracted by a noise coming from the other side of the auditorium. The concert hall's ticket seller has set up his box office window in the aisle, and he is loudly conducting business without regard for the music onstage. The performers on the stage don't seem to notice him either.

Next, you hear an argument coming from the rear of the auditorium. An audience member is yelling at an usher, saying that he wants his money back, and the usher is officiously telling him that the house policy is to give no refunds. The musicians, the workman, the ticket seller and the usher are all oblivious of each other.

What would your impression of this concert be? Would you be able to enjoy the music, despite the distractions?

What's really going on in this story?

The orchestra intended for you to have a certain kind of experience, but you had a completely different experience than what they had planned for you. They wanted you to hear an evening of beautiful music; your experience included not only their music, but also the distractions coming from all over the auditorium. To each of the players in this story—the conductor, the musicians, the workman, the ticket seller and the usher, the evening was going just fine. Each of them was doing his or her job, and none of them realized that, from your perspective, the concert was a mess.

So, what does this story have to do with branding and marketing?

Here's what I believe: The performances most companies put on for their customers resemble this concert more closely than those companies would either recognize or admit.

Imagine that the conductor and the orchestra represent a product's advertising—well crafted, well performed, designed to connect emotionally with the audience. But advertising is rarely the only thing the customer 'hears' from a product.

Think of the workman, creating the noise that distracted you from the music. How often have a company's operational systems, glitches and inconveniences gotten in the way when you tried to buy, use or learn about their products? Have you ever waited on hold for 15 minutes because the company you're calling doesn't have enough people to answer phones, or waited on a hot plane during a maintenance delay? Who hasn't used a website with cumbersome navigation?

Next, think of the ticket seller selling tickets during the concert. How often has the actual process of buying a product influenced your opinions about that product, for better or worse? Was it difficult to compare two models of the product? Was it hard to determine the true price of a complex product, like a car or a vacation? Did the seller make it easy to buy or difficult to buy?

And what about the usher, hiding behind the protective cover of bureaucracy as she spouted policy to a disgruntled customer? When was the last time your opinion of a product was colored by poor customer service like this? Yesterday? Was it really that long ago?

All of these types of experiences contribute to the impressions customers have of products. Advertising, brochures, direct mail and other sales pitches have no special privilege when it comes to helping customers form opinions about a product—as far as a customer is concerned, any interaction with a product is a 'marketing' interaction.

Consider the way someone's opinion of a car is formed. Advertising, brochures and sales pitches contribute to the customer's impression of the car, but they are in no way the major factors forming her opinion. Seeing the car on the road, reading comments in the press, hearing the way the dealership's service

Many Inputs

Advertising
Comments in the press
Brochures
Meet the manager
Salespeople
See the service department
Comments from friends
Purchase process
Seeing the car on the road
Dealer receptionist
Website
Financing process
Test drive

Meet Ruth. She wants to buy a new car.

Figure 1. **Brand Impression of a Car**

department interacts with other customers—each of these help the customer form her *brand impression* of the car and the dealership. Just like your experience at the orchestra concert, the beautiful music of advertising plays only a partial role in the creation of the customer's brand impression.

A friend of mine had an experience with Kmart that illustrates a real–world example of this process. She hadn't been to Kmart in a while, but was familiar with their advertising, which promised products by Martha Stewart and Jaclyn Smith. Arriving at a Kmart with these images in mind, she was greeted at the entrance by loud rap music playing on a boombox. She noticed soft drink cases piled high to the ceiling; products throughout the store were scattered on half-empty, dusty shelves, and she had a hard time finding a salesperson to answer her questions. She commented that the experience in the store had nothing to do with the promises in the ads. My friend may have initially reacted positively to Kmart's advertising, but her experience in the store quickly erased any positive impressions she had. In the place of these positive impressions, she created new, negative impressions of Kmart in her mind. This experience redefined the Kmart brand for her.

> *Your brand is not what you say you are... Your brand is what your customers think you are.*

A Brand is a Thought

A brand is not simply the message a marketer intends to send to a customer. A brand is the message the customer perceives about the product, which may be something altogether different than the message the marketer intended to send. Similar to the orchestra concert, Kmart's ads intended to tell my friend one thing, but her experiences caused her to think something else.

Your brand is not something you can hold, or touch, or see. You can't send it through the mail or project it on the airwaves. Your brand is a thought in your customer's mind, which she creates at her own discretion as she interacts with your company and your product. No matter how great a product's advertising is—or, for that matter, how great the product is—the customer still reserves the right to make her own decision about how to think about the product. Just like the orchestra members, oblivious to the gap between what they are trying to communicate and what the audience is actually hearing, most companies fail to recognize that what they say about themselves may not be the same as what people think about them.

Being Understood

*"There are three poems in every poem.
The poem the poet intends, the poem that ends up on paper, and the poem that the reader understands."*

This was an insight from a friend's high school English teacher as that friend searched for her voice and style as a writer. Now a successful author, she has shared this insight with me. It is a meaningful marketing lesson.

In human communication, there is often a wide chasm between intention and perception. The poem that ends up on paper doesn't always translate the poet's intentions in a way that helps the reader understand those intentions. And the meaning of a poem—or a marketing message—is worth nothing, save self-indulgence, if its intentions are not understood.

Great marketing and branding are about closing this gap between intention and perception. They are not about telling a story. They are about having our stories understood.

Customers do not want to be told how to think about a product. They reserve that right for themselves. You can coax, cajole, persuade and plead, but at the end of the day customers will form their thoughts about your product on their own. By recognizing that the role of marketing and branding are not to tell a story, but to make sure that a story is understood, we will aim much higher in our communications with customers, taking nothing for granted. We won't look at marketing communication as a process of making declarations, pronouncements or proclamations; we won't

You can lead a horse to water, but you can't make him think.

assume we can tell people what to think about our products. We will instead look at marketing as a process of making it possible for customers to tell themselves what to think about our products.

Another friend recently forwarded a postcard to me from a company announcing a corporate name change. The headline on the card read:

**Interim Career Consulting
is rebranding as Spherion.**

My friend circled the headline and scrawled the following note on the card: "That's it, that's all there is to it. Just tell the world you're branded and you're branded. Steve, looks like you're out of a job."

Wouldn't things be different if life were so easy?

Spherion's claim is ludicrous because it assumes that a company can just declare what its brand is, at its own discretion. It's as if they are saying, "Here's what we came up with for our brand. This is how you should think about us now." Spherion's view of branding, like most popular branding concepts, regards the customer as a passive participant to whom the brand is unveiled after its creation. By the time the customer gets involved, according to this model of branding, the brand is complete. The brand is assumed to be iconic and immutable, much like the statue of a dead general, which is designed in the artist's studio, cast by a skilled craftsman, and then unveiled and displayed in the town square in hopes of impressing everyone as they go by.

There's a really big problem with this idea of branding —it doesn't describe how things actually work in the real world. **Customers**

are anything but passive participants in the branding process. However solid and well-chiseled a finely crafted brand message may seem, it becomes putty as soon as it enters a customer's mind and is molded to fit both into that customer's current view of the product and of the world as a whole. A customer relates every new brand message to all of her previous encounters with the product, and then decides which ones are most important to forming her opinion, ignoring or discounting the rest. She then filters her experience of these encounters through her own personal biases, perceptions and perspectives, creating a highly personal and unique view of the brand. By the time she's finished creating it, her brand impression may bear little (if any) resemblance to the marketer's intention. It is truly *her* brand impression.

> *Branding isn't something companies do to their customers. Branding is something customers do to companies and their products.*

Think of an airline and its relationship with its customers. Frequent flyers tend to have strong opinions about the airlines they do business with. They can describe the airline's capabilities and personality with rich detail, and can articulate their preferences among brands very clearly. The reasons for a customer's particular beliefs about an airline are a cumulative sum of hundreds, if not thousands, of contacts that customer has had with the airline, very few of which directly involve the work product of the marketing department. Exposure to the airline's advertising may influence a piece of the customer's brand opinion, but it is only one of the many product experiences that the customer considers when evaluating the product. As the customer collects these experiences, she is actively engaged in forming her personal brand impression of the airline.

Contrary to the traditional view, branding is not something that companies do to their customers. Branding is actually something that customers do to companies and products. This represents an important 180-degree flip in the way most people look at branding. The marketing activities of most companies do not take into account the active role that customers play in creating their own personal brand impressions.

Branding is Inevitable

I once was hired by the marketing department of a company to develop a brand strategy. They brought me to meet the company president, who said, "This sounds good, Steve, but, I have to tell you, I haven't even decided yet if we need to have a brand."

My answer: "Too late. Every time people interact with you, they create thoughts and opinions about you. You already have a brand, whether you like it or not. The only thing you should worry about now is what kind of brand you would like to have."

Branding is not a discretionary act. A company president may decide not to "have a brand," but that wouldn't stop his customers from branding his company.

Branding is Everybody's Business

And branding isn't just an inevitable phenomenon for big companies. Any product, no matter how small, gets branded as its customers or potential customers come in contact with it. That project proposal you sent to your largest customer – it's getting branded by her right now as she's reading it. What about the corner Italian restaurant near your house? Your brand impression of it might be much stronger than your impression of a large national Italian restaurant chain, like Olive Garden. That job candidate you interviewed yesterday? You branded him within 5 minutes of meeting him.

The impact of Tom Peters' landmark cover story in the August, 1997 issue of *Fast Company*, "The Brand Called You," went well beyond the fact that it encouraged people to see themselves as brands. It also helped people see that branding wasn't just something that big companies do with big advertising campaigns. Everything gets branded, inevitably.

So why should we care about all of this? Why does it matter? Is branding just about image, identity and reputation? Or does it go deeper?

2

How Brand Impressions Are Formed...and Why it Matters

Everything is Marketing

To answer the questions posed at the end of the last chapter, let's go back to the example of the car and see how these principles affect a customer's choice about which car to buy (Figure 2).

Let's imagine a woman named Ruth who is shopping for a new car. Let's also assume that she is choosing between VW's New Beetle, the Honda Accord and the Toyota Camry.

Ruth first learned about the New Beetle by seeing the car on the road. It immediately evoked memories of riding in the back seat of her aunt's Beetle with her cousin when they were kids. Shortly thereafter, she saw an ad for the car in a magazine, and then she started to notice that people were talking about it. Her local newspaper's automotive editor wrote a story on the car, which she read. By this point her interest was piqued, so she stopped by a dealership and picked up a brochure.

While driving out of the VW dealership she decided to pull into the Honda dealership next door and check out the Accord. Her best friend was a loyal Honda owner, and had encouraged her to think seriously about buying one of their cars. Unlike the VW dealership, where she had managed to escape before being noticed by a sales-person, she was immediately accosted in the Honda dealership by a polyester-clad guy named Bruce. Although she felt a little pressured by his overly familiar sales approach, she agreed to take a test drive. The car was comfortable, but she didn't feel that comfortable around Bruce.

That night she went to the VW, Honda and Toyota websites. She was a little annoyed that it was hard to find good pictures of the Beetle on VW's site, and she liked the way Honda let her calculate the price of her car with different features. She got bored after a few minutes on the Toyota website and left to buy a book on amazon.com. On the following Saturday, she test-drove the VW and the Toyota, clutching her newspaper's automotive section, which contained ads for all three cars. As she drove the Toyota, she thought it was fun to drive, and she liked its practical features. As she was leaving the Toyota dealership, she noticed a customer having an argument with a sales manager. Although she had liked the Accord, she remembered how she had been uncomfortable riding as a passenger in her friend's car.

Ruth's brand impressions of all three cars were evolving simultaneously. At some moments, the Toyota seemed like the right car for her, and at other times the Honda was in first place. Her mind

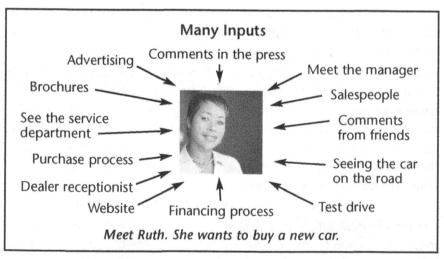

Figure 2. **Brand Impression of a Car**

kept returning to the VW, which she thought was cute and fun, but she felt a need to guard against letting nostalgia get in the way of practicality. Brand impressions of each car were percolating simultaneously in her thoughts as she considered the experiences she had with each car—the ads she saw, the brochures, the websites, the salespeople, test-driving the cars, comments she heard from friends. As she weighed all of these different experiences and thoughts, an overall composite feeling for each car was forming in her brain.

And then, the moment of truth: Ruth thought to herself, "The VW is best for me. This is the one I want." She had made up her mind.

The Connection Between Experience and Action

This decision to buy the VW over the Toyota or the Honda was fueled by the wide variety of experiences and interactions Ruth had with each car. As she weighed all of these experiences, cumulative impressions were forming of each car. The overall impression of the VW won out over the others.

Ruth's brand impressions—the overall thoughts and feelings she had for each car –directly affected her purchase decision. The sum total of experiences with the VW added up to a winning formula, relative to the other cars. In

Branding isn't about "getting your name out" in the marketplace... Branding is about getting an individual customer to say "I want it!"

this story, there was a direct connection between the entire set of experiences Ruth had with each product and which dealership made the sale.

Celebrity is Overrated

Branding is often thought of as the process of creating awareness and identity for a product. As Ruth's story shows us, branding goes far beyond this. Branding isn't just about your product's celebrity status in the marketplace. It's about the direct connection between what a customer thinks about your product and what that customer decides to do in relation to your product. It's about how customers decide to choose one product over another. It's about how you compete for customers. It's about how you succeed.

Every single interaction a customer has with a product has the potential to strengthen or dilute the customer's brand impression. When you consider this, it's easy to see how product experiences that resemble the cacophonous orchestra concert can destroy a company's ability to sell its product. As we can see in Figure 3, there is a direct connection between these experiences and your product's success:

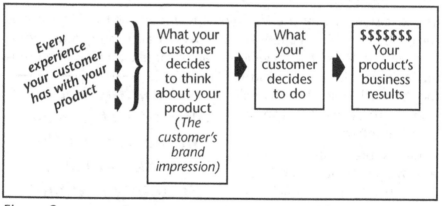

Figure 3.

The total set of experiences customers have with a product drives brand impressions, which in turn drive the customer behaviors that fuel results. The challenge is to *orchestrate* these experiences in a way that leads customers to create brand impressions that encourage the action you are looking for. If you are able to do this, you improve the performance results of your product.

How often does exposure to marketing stimuli encourage customers to act in the way the marketers hope they will act? Unfortunately, the most common reaction people have to marketing stimuli is *not* to act. In his book, *Data Smog*, David Shenk estimates that the average American is exposed to more than 3000 advertising messages per day. Even if he's wrong, and it's really only 300 messages per day, it's clear that, unless you have Compulsive Shopping Disorder, you are ignoring virtually all advertising messages to which we are exposed. And any product that presented you with a series of disjointed, conflicting messages, reminiscent of the orchestra parable, would have no chance of getting your attention.

Dealing with the Noise

Your customers live their lives awash in a sea of marketing cacophony, overwhelmed by the sales pitches competing for their money and attention. Here's an ironic way that BoatingChannel.com uses this situation in their solicitation for advertising, estimating advertising exposures to be much higher than Shenk's number:

> Repetition is critical to a successful advertising campaign. It takes time for a message to sink in because the average American is exposed to 10,000 advertising messages per day—That's a lot of messages for the human brain to process. And, even though your ad will be going to an audience predisposed to a boating vacation, they may not be in the market for your service the week they get your ad, or they may be in the early stages of decision making...The point is it will take time for your message to sink in—for people to remember that you have the vacation experience they are looking for.[1]

If I were a seller of boating vacations, reading that would hardly convince me to advertise! It would lead me to believe that any money spent advertising my product would be wasted, with my ads disappearing like a drop of water in the ocean.

In an article on systemic thinking[2], Daniel Aronson, describes what happens when we are confronted with more information than we can possibly process:

> While we need to take in information to act, the richness of the environment means that processing all available information is

impossible—there is simply too much of it. Reducing the tremendous amount of input from the environment requires that two things happen to the stream of information provided us by the environment:

- It has to be condensed
- It has to be structured to reveal the linkages between different elements.

This is what happens with product experiences. In order to make sense of multiple experiences with one product, we sort the information into categories and process data in larger chunks, which "serve to condense experience from a string of unique stimuli into sets of similar experiences."[3] As customers, we create these categories in our minds and use them to organize our thoughts, accomplishing the task which Aronson describes above, condensing information and structuring it in a way that enables us to deal with a large set of product experiences.

For example, when evaluating cars, Ruth considered hundreds of different pieces of information. To deal with this, she might have grouped all of her thoughts about a car's interior into one category, all thoughts about the feel of the car's handling into another, and all thoughts about the salesman into a different one. This way, she was able to organize her thoughts into a manageable set.

As new information came in about a particular car, it may or may not have fit into existing categories. If it fit, and was consistent with her existing thoughts in that category, the beliefs she had about that category were reinforced, e.g., an article she read about the car's ability to take tight turns might have reinforced the personal experience Ruth had during the test drive. If the new information fit into an issue category but was inconsistent with what she already believed about that issue, then she would have needed to reassess her beliefs about it, e.g., if a friend who bought from the same dealership had told her that he thinks the salesman was trustworthy, conflicting with her previous view of this man's integrity. As she gathered experiences with the cars she was considering, Ruth was continually organizing and discarding data, forming her personal brand impressions.

Do You Hear What I Hear?

Back in the 50's or 60's, most people probably had a pretty similar set of experiences with Coca-Cola. There was one kind of Coke, it was sold and served in only a couple of ways, and TV advertising was the company's prime vehicle, other than the product itself, for telling us about the product. But now, Coke comes in many different varieties and sizes, we can buy it in many different ways, and there are many different ways we can learn about the product. It is now more likely that each of us has our own personal set of experiences with Coca-Cola.

This is true for most products, many to a much greater extent than Coke. Our personal experiences with products are unique to each of us, giving each of us a different set of ingredients with which to form our brand impressions. Consider a hotel chain. You may have stayed in five of their hotels and I may have stayed in six of them. Your stays may have all been for business trips, while I may have stayed in three hotels for business, one hotel while attending a convention, and two others for vacations. You may have had a travel agent book your rooms and I may have called the chain's 800 number. You may have had helpful front desk agents and terrible meals, while I may have encountered surly check-in clerks and exceptional in-room dining. We each have our own personal set of experiences with this product.

> *Each person's experience with a product is as unique as a snowflake. Each of us has a personal experience that is experienced by no other individual.*

This unique set of personal product experiences forms the 'raw ingredients' from which customers create brand impressions. Because each person's inventory of experiences is unique, it is possible that each customer could create a unique, personal brand impression. Every new experience a customer has, whether it is with a customer service representative or with the product itself, enriches and personalizes the customer's brand impression, making it more his own. Traditional views of branding that are based on communicating the same message to many customers don't reflect the actual way customers interact with and evaluate products.

Through the Looking Glass: The Filter of Personal Perception

Everybody Thinks Something Different

The unique set of experiences each customer has with a product is not the only reason that each customer can potentially have a unique, personal brand impression. Another reason is the intensely personal way that each customer perceives and processes these experiences.

Let's look at three reasons why the process of perceiving product experiences steers customers further away from the herd, to personal brand impressions:

I. **The Importance A Customer Assigns to Each Product Interaction is Completely Subjective.**

    We constantly make choices about which stimuli in our environment deserve our attention, and which should be ignored. As you read this, I trust your focus is on these words and you are not paying attention to the feeling of your shirt on your back, or to the slight squeeze your socks are exerting on your calves. Those stimuli are reaching your brain—but you have chosen to ignore them. Similarly, at a party you are able to shut out much of the conversation around you and focus on the person with whom you are currently speaking. Human beings have the interesting quality of being, simultaneously, infinitely distractible yet capable of ignoring most of the world around them.

    Also, there are many things which we don't ignore, but which we decide to classify as unimportant. A three pack a day smoker can't ignore his cough, but he sure can tell himself it isn't such a big deal. We allow ourselves a very permissive prerogative to assign whatever importance we like to the things we think about. When it comes to products, customers are faced with many product experiences from which to form brand impressions, and each customer has the power to decide how much importance to assign to each of these experiences.

Some people may put much stock in advertising messages when evaluating a product, and some may consider the input from advertising to be relatively unimportant. Some customers pay attention to what their friends say, while some will only buy a product if they can try it with their own hands. In any event, it is the customer's choice to consider or ignore any experience he has with a product, and then to assign whatever importance suits him to the experiences that he does choose to consider.

By running a heavy schedule of advertising, a company is trying to stack the deck in its favor by increasing the weight of messages that reinforce the brand impression the company wants customers to have. But, no matter how much noise the advertising creates, it doesn't always seem louder to the customer. Here's an example: You've seen hundreds of McDonald's commercials, and you've eaten there many times. Imagine that on your next trip the bathroom is filthy. Now, you get to decide how much the dirty bathroom colors your impression of the brand. A product experience can be a much louder "marketing message" than an ad in a customer's mind.[4] It's up to the customer to decide.

2. Inference and Mistaken Completeness

People usually think they have a greater portion of the available information about a subject than they really do. We have a strong tendency to extrapolate from limited, incomplete information to what we believe is a comprehensive view of something. I call this process of inference "mistaken completeness." It affects how we form our opinions on issues in the news and how we get to know people, to name a few examples, but it also happens as we gather information on products.

A participant in a focus group I was moderating told of a hotel stay during which he had noticed a certain paper cup on the floor of the hotel's parking garage during the entire 5 days he was at the hotel. He made a very confident statement: "If the hotel can't manage to pick up a paper cup off the floor for 5 days, all I can believe is that they are too incompetent to run a big hotel efficiently." A customer, with limited information, is prepared to extrapolate from highly specific instances to comprehensive opinions.

An article on Internet privacy by Jeffrey Rosen in the April 30, 2000 *New York Times Magazine* described this phenomenon in terms of how incomplete personal information can distort our views of a person. Rosen's argument translates well to our conversation about branding:

> There are many fearful consequences to the loss of privacy, but none perhaps more disquieting than this: privacy protects us from being misdefined and judged out of context. When your browsing habits or e-mail messages are exposed to strangers, you may be reduced, in their eyes, to nothing more than the most salacious book you once read or the most vulgar joke you once told. And even if your Internet browsing isn't in any way embarrassing, you run the risk of being stereotyped as the kind of person who would read a particular book or listen to a particular song. Your public identity may be distorted by fragments of information that have little to do with how you define yourself. In a world where citizens are bombarded with information, people form impressions quickly, based on sound bites, and these brief impressions tend to oversimplify and misrepresent our complicated and often contradictory characters.[5]

It is easy for people or products to be misdefined if those who form opinions about them have limited information. They don't always realize—or care—how limited their information is.

Think how the phenomenon of mistaken completeness out-wits you when you meet a new person. If the first thing you hear a person say is insightful, you have a tendency to think of the person as being pretty smart. On the other hand, if the first thing they say is kind of stupid, you may 'brand' that person as an intellectual lightweight, even if the first comment you heard was an aberration or was taken out of context. First impres-sions aren't always fair, but they are powerful because they are, at that time, the only information we have on which to make a judgment. And they are often inaccurate—how often does love at first sight end up being love for life?

Mistaken completeness can also work to your advantage. The first week of business school at Northwestern University's Kellogg Graduate School of Management in the fall of 1983 was a tense, pressure-filled time of self-doubt and anxiety for me and my classmates. The core introductory class, Business Policy, was a strategy course taught by Professor Lawrence Lavengood, who had been teaching since my father went to Northwestern thirty years before. Professor Lavengood remind-ed my friends and me of Professor Kingsfield from the movie *The Paper Chase,* ready to expose publicly any intellectual weakness or shoddy thinking. Our postures were a nervous mixture of faked poise and attempts to remain inconspicuous, since humiliation lurked like the angel of death in the air of the classroom, ready to pounce on the first victim who said some-thing stupid.

Our first paper was a two page analysis of a simple case study. Somehow serendipity caused me to write something that Lavengood really liked, and he chose to read it to the class as an example of the kind of insights we should all strive for.

Yes, it was mostly dumb luck. My class was filled with incred-ible people, many of whom have since built notable careers, but I was instantly branded in my classmates' minds as a 'smart guy,' based solely on Lavengood's favorable review. My class-mates had only known me for a few days, so they really didn't *know* me. So they took the little information they had and, by inference, extrapolated a more complete view of me. Thank you, Professor Lavengood.

Mistaken completeness is an important feature of the process of branding. A customer will form an opinion of a brand by using some or all of the information she has at hand. Despite the fact that many product experiences will be used to form a brand impression, these will, in virtually all cases, be only a small portion of all possible product experiences. The information is, then, inherently incomplete. But the customer is rarely willing, prepared or motivated to expend energy to fill in gaps in her information, except if she is researching an imminent transaction or has a strong interest in the product. Instead, she makes do with what she has and infers the whole from an incomplete set of parts. We can't expect customers to work very hard to fill in the gaps in their limited information, or, for that matter, even to recognize that their information is limited.

3. The Prism of Perception

An inherent fact of human life is that people can look at the same thing and have completely different impressions or opinions of it. Turn on the TV or flip through a news magazine, and you will see that the grist for content is human disagreement, be it political news, art criticism, sitcoms or pulp TV talk shows.

Why is this?

Everything we see is colored by our own perception. We don't see things as they are, but, more specifically, as we think they are.

Everything is subjective. Everything. Think of this: our eyes and the optic centers in our brains actually visualize the world around us upside-down, but our brains are programmed to invert everything we see back to an upright position so that we see the world right side up. Everything we see is a function of our perception, even if we are not aware of the way our brain is filtering the outside world.

Customers filter everything they think about products through their own personal prism of perception. Think of how differently your friends, colleagues and acquaintances approach the world. Is it any surprise to realize that they react in their own individual ways to products and marketing messages?

Branding is a tricky business. Customers, who are continually bombarded with marketing messages, consider any and all experiences with products as they evaluate those products. Each customer has a unique set of experiences with a given product, and has complete discretion about how to interpret those experiences. Despite this messy, complex situation, the stakes are high, because brand impressions directly influence customers to behave in a way that affects the product's performance results. How do most organizations approach this situation?

3

Brute Force Branding... and Why it Doesn't Work

Bigger, Louder, More Clever. Who Cares?

Like many people, my first images of the word 'brand' were associated with cowboys, molten metal and helpless cows. As a kid I learned how ranchers take red-hot iron to the skin of their livestock to imprint the ranch's identifying logo on the animal. I can still recall the films we saw in school; calves held in place by men in chaps while the brand is applied, the young animal's face writhing in pain. As soon as the operation is complete, the calf tries to run away, only to realize that it is penned in with nowhere to escape. Kicking up hot Texas dust, it runs helplessly in circles.

I think that the prevalent view of the branding of products looks a lot more like the branding of cows than most people would like to admit. Like cowboys forcibly imprinting a permanent, indelible mark on a powerless calf, marketers think they have the power to "brand" their products into customer's brains.

On the ranch, the cowboy holds all the power in the transaction. One minute the cow is peacefully chewing his cud, the next he has been told—in no uncertain terms—what his branded identity is. Substitute a big advertising campaign for a red-hot branding iron, and this pretty much describes the dominant view of branding over the last 50 years. But in the new world of branding we've described, customers are not nearly as helpless as cows, and marketers are nowhere near as powerful as cowboys.

Unfortunately, most "marketing cowboys" think they still have powerful branding irons at their disposal. Consider how most branding projects take place. Here's the way an ad agency team might discuss a new branding assignment...

Account Executive: Thanks for coming to the meeting. We're here to discuss the client's assignment to create a brand for their new widget. They'll have lots of competition, so we need some really powerful advertising if we ever hope to get noticed.

Creative Director: It's time for some breakthrough creative thinking. John, any great design ideas?

Art Director: Yes...I'm thinking of bold colors and use of stark geometric shapes to help us cut through the clutter. We need to be on the leading edge of design to get noticed in today's world.

Copywriter: I've started working on catchy taglines. I'm thinking that a humorous approach will work best.

Account Executive: Or maybe a celebrity spokesperson.

Copywriter: Axl Rose would be perfect! How could someone not notice him?

Media Planner: And we'll have to get in front of the target audience as much as possible. How big is our budget?

Account Executive: We're in luck. The client really wants us to make a loud noise in the marketplace. We've got $10 million to spend in the next 6 months.

Media Planner: Alright! We should be able to get 9 or 10 impressions for every member of the target audience.

I'm exaggerating...but just a little bit. I have sat through hundreds of branding discussions over the last 20 years, and this little scene is representative of what typically passes for brand development. What these ad agency guys are essentially saying in this discussion is, "If we have a really powerful message to interrupt our customers with, and we interrupt them with it enough times, they will be branded." This is like saying, "If I have a really big stick, and I hit you over the head with it enough times, you will eventually agree with me."

I like to call this view of branding "Brute Force Branding." It assumes that we can muscle our way into our customers' minds. It assumes that the bigger ad budget and the best creative staff wins.

What counts in the brute force branding process is the ability to grab a customer's attention and inform her what she is supposed to think about the product.

Most marketing plans based on brute force branding focus on powerful communication media such as advertising, promotion and direct mail to catch customers' attention and create brand impressions. The more 'granular' product experiences that happen in the course of a customer's ongoing interactions with a product—the behavior of a hotel front desk clerk, the product knowledge of a retail sales clerk, the way an owner's manual reads—are usually not considered as "media" in the brute force branding process.

Will Brute Force Branding Work in Today's World?

Although brute force branding has been the dominant branding concept in our lifetimes, it is actually a very new phenomenon. Throughout the entire 10,000 years of recorded human civilization, it is only for a portion of the 20th century that sellers attempted to persuade people to buy their products by interrupting them as they go about their daily lives. Brute force branding may have worked for a brief moment of human history, but it increasingly ineffective in today's world. The customer of today is too savvy, self-reliant and skeptical to fall for brute force branding in all but the most special circumstances.

The last few decades have seen a relentless, tectonic shift in power from people who sell things to people who buy things. We live in an age of customer power, an age where customers are less gullible and more difficult to persuade.

This rise in customer power has been driven by four trends:

1. **Customers have more choices than ever before.**

Recently, I left a downtown Chicago meeting and headed for suburban Deerfield. I needed to buy a backpack and could have stopped at any of five different stores on my way home. I arbitrarily chose Sportmart and, once inside, I was able to choose from more than

> *A major shift in power from sellers to buyers*

100 backpacks covering an entire wall. Product proliferation means that for every product I decide to buy, I get to say "no" to numerous other products. Don't you love having that power?

2. **Customers have access to plentiful, objective information.**

In addition to our friends' recommendations, we used to depend mostly on advertising or the claims of salespeople for product information. Now it is easy to find tens, or even hundreds, of objective reviews about a product we'd like to buy, and we can use the Internet to share information with our friends like we never could before. The last time I was car shopping, a Volvo salesman told me that his car is much safer than his Swedish competitor, Saab. I knew better, because I had looked up crash test data before leaving the house. Knowledge can be empowering—if you're the one who has it!

3. **Customers control a valuable resource that sellers want: information about themselves.**

In an earlier age, driven by advertising and limited product choices, sellers didn't have to know much about individual buyers. After all, the mass media that were used to communicate product messages, such as TV and magazines, couldn't distinguish between individual customers. And even if they could, it wouldn't have mattered very much because sellers weren't prepared to say or sell different things to different people. But in today's age of one to one marketing, product proliferation, mass customization of products and personal brand impressions, sellers can use personal information about a customer to gain a competitive edge by personalizing service to customers in a way a competitor can't match. When an airline asks you for your seat and meal preferences and the vacation destinations that most interest you, they aren't asking just to be nice. They are looking for a way to serve you that will increase your loyalty to them over the competition. The information you provide has a value to them that gives you, the customer, power in the relationship.

4. **Customers trust others less and themselves more.**

    Can you imagine the American public today falling for the McCarthy hearings the way we did 50 years ago? No way! The events of the intervening years, such as Vietnam, Watergate, the Enron/Andersen fiasco and the constant media exposure of dishonest lawyers, journalists, politicians and CEO's, have deflated the respect we have for those in positions of authority. Our trust in ourselves has remained high, but our trust in those who sell us things, give us advice or make rules for us has declined considerably.

    As customers have become more savvy, skeptical, cynical, and self-reliant, they don't believe everything they are told, especially from people trying to sell them things. They believe in themselves. They believe in their own individuality.

    Figure 4, prepared from data included in the Yesawich, Pepperdine, Brown & Russell/Yankelovich Partners National Travel Monitor study, illustrates this in a clear way. Note how much our confidence in things like journalism and medicine, always considered objective and authoritative, has diminished.

Why has our trust in these items dwindled? It is not so much that they have become less trustworthy. The more important issue

Consumer Attitudes **Confidence & Trust**		
Great confidence in:	1987 (%)	2003 (%)
My own abilities	80%	86%
News reports on TV	54	27
News reports in newspapers	49	25*
News reports in magazines	37	14*
Recommendations of doctors	69	65
Recommendations of travel agents	34	26*
Advice from religious leaders	N/A	37
Salespeople in clothing stores	23	7
Federal government	N/A	12
Corp. point of view advert./statements	20	3*
Advertising	8	3*
Used car salesman	15	2

Source: Yesawich, Pepperdine, Brown & Russell/Yankelovich Partners 2003 National Travel Monitor.   * 2002 data

Figure 4. **The only item with lower trust than advertising is used car salesmen**

is that we have become less trusting. Who do you trust more, yourself or the claim made by a TV commercial?

This is a New Customer!!!!

Every decision we make about marketing and branding has to start with the recognition that we are dealing with an empowered customer who doesn't behave or believe like her grandmother. Today's savvy, self-confident, self-reliant, cynical customer believes in noth-

> *For today's customer, scrutiny is very high, and tolerance is very low.*

ing more than her own individuality. Empowered further by a teeming choice of products fighting for her attention, and armed with plenty of objective information about those products, today's customer has decided to be much more demanding, discerning, judgmental, impatient and critical, and much less loyal, trusting or committed.

So, how will this newly empowered customer react to brute force branding? Is this the kind of person who can be told how to think, just by bombarding her with frequent, clever ads?

I don't think so.

The idea that brute force alone can drive purchase behavior and build brand loyalty is an anachronism. Today's customer wants to make his own choices about how to think about products. He is less gullible than earlier generations, and sheer force alone will not move him. And he has been assailed with advertising messages so frequently and for so many years that he has tuned out and said, "Stop. I'm not listening." With notable exceptions, brute force branding is not a workable model in today's marketplace.

A look at those notable exceptions helps make that case. Yes, Budweiser and Nike rely on a lot of brute force to build their brands. And maybe you could too, if you had billions of dollars and Michael Jordan, as Nike does. But Budweiser and Nike represent a very small share of the marketplace. It's unfortunate that people always use big companies as a frame of reference for studying branding, since most of us are involved with products that operate on a much smaller scale and will never have occasion to use television advertising for brand building. Once you get down to the level of most business-es—corner cafes, small manufacturers, law firms with 4 partners—it's easy to see that the television/tagline/ logo/me/me/me chest beating of brute force branding doesn't work. And even among big companies with big marketing budgets, Nike, Budweiser and McDonald's are exceptions. There are very few products, no matter how well funded, who can rely on a brute force advertising-driven approach to build strong brands. How many times has a television commercial come on for a financial services company and you recognize the music from the commercial but can't remember what company it is promoting? The company's brute force approach hasn't worked, because you haven't let it. It takes a lot more than great advertising for you to let a product into your life.

Brute force branding has seen its better days and no longer deserves to be considered as the primary means for branding products. Has the world of marketing recognized this?

For the most part, no.

Marketing and branding is still most frequently practiced in a brute force way that assumes a relatively powerless customer. Marketers interrupt customers with hundreds of advertising messages everyday, a system that is very convenient for marketers but hardly optimal for customers. Direct marketing programs are considered successful if 'only' 98% of people throw away the mail they receive. Marketers act with impunity, as if there were no repercussions for this abuse of customers' time, attention and trash cans.

This increase in customer power caught the world of marketing off-guard. Customers started saying, "prove it" while marketers were still saying, "order today!" And customers were asking "what's in it for me?" while marketers were still saying "new and improved!" Oops.

It's as if you began playing a weekly tennis game with the 10-year old kid next door, beating him easily each time you played. All of the sudden, after many years, he catches you off-guard and beats you. In your complacency you have missed his growing up, and in that one moment you realize that he has become both an adult and an equal on the court.

But now, our customers have grown up, without the marketing world noticing or changing the practice of marketing to reflect their new "adult" mindset. Enjoying their newfound power, they will not be easily sold, cajoled, impressed or persuaded by smoke and mirrors. For these new customers, scrutiny is high and tolerance is low. We need to change the way we interact with them, or our marketing messages will seem irrelevant.

So if brute force doesn't create strong brand impressions, what does?

4

Brand Harmony

What Does It Sound Like to be Your Customer?

What makes your brand impressions of products or services strong?

Clearly, some of your brand impressions are stronger than others. There are some products or services that have a very clear identity in your mind, yet there are many others for which you have only vague, fuzzy feelings.

A brand impression is strong if it gives the customer a clear idea of why she wants to be involved with the product being branded. In essence, she is saying, "I get it—I understand what this product can do for me—and I want it." She not only understands the message, but she finds it meaningful and wants to act on the feeling the brand impression gives her.

How does a customer come to perceive a product's messages as clear, meaningful and motivating?

Let's look back at Ruth's experiences with the VW Beetle (Figure 5). We described earlier how Ruth's decision to buy the VW was driven by all of the experiences she had with VW—including ads, salespeople, seeing and driving the car and every other interaction with the product.

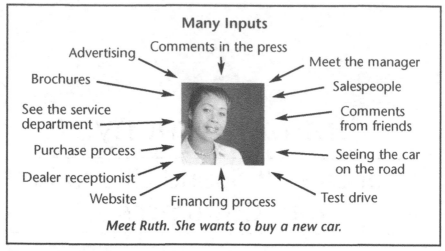

Many Inputs

Advertising — Comments in the press

Brochures —

See the service department —

Purchase process —

Dealer receptionist —

Website — Financing process

Meet the manager

Salespeople

Comments from friends

Seeing the car on the road

Test drive

Meet Ruth. She wants to buy a new car.

Figure 5. **Brand Impression of a Car**

How did all of these experiences blend together in Ruth's mind?

Was there a *harmony* in the way they blended, or did Ruth perceive a *dissonance* among these experiences?

Were the experiences *mutually reinforcing?* Did they tell a *cumulative story?* Or was it a *jumbled mess?*

Brand Harmony

The way various experiences with a product blend in a customer's mind creates **Brand Harmony.** If different experiences with a product blend well together, there will be a strong harmony and the customer will be more likely to form a solid overall brand impression of the product. If the customer's experiences with the product seem disjointed, unrelated or con-

> *Brand Harmony says blending, not brute force, creates strong brand impressions*

flicting, there will be a dissonance and the customer will most likely have an impression similar to that of the audience in our orchestra parable.

This is not to say, by any means, that advertising is an ineffective marketing medium. What it does say is that the effectiveness of advertising is not a function of its brute force, but of how well the advertising blends with the other experiences the customer has with the product. 'Great advertising' that doesn't resonate with everything else the customer experiences isn't great advertising.

In their book, *Making Connections: Teaching and the Human Brain,* (Association for Supervision and Curriculum Development, Alexandria, Virginia, 1991), Renate Nummela Caine and Geoffrey Caine describe how various pieces of information can reinforce each other and aid learning. The Caines write that "the brain is designed to perceive and generate patterns, and it resists having meaningless patterns imposed on it." (p81) They describe how we create "thematic maps" that help us understand how pieces of information are linked together. Thematic maps with strong connections "become meaningful very quickly, by virtue of their being packaged in relevant, complex, and highly socially interactive experiences."

Educators know that they can help students learn better if they teach a subject by presenting information in a number of different contexts. As the student begins to perceive patterns and connections between different pieces of information, he begins to comprehend the material. The same dynamic is at work if customers perceive a resonance between the different experiences they have with a product. Strong Brand Harmony makes it easier to understand a product's message.

Additionally, the Caines write that strong connections between pieces of information stored in thematic maps create a strong "indexing function" that makes it easier to recall relevant information. Conversely, if the connections are not strong, "information can only be called up in limited ways and is very inflexible." Similarly, strong Brand Harmony makes it easier to remember a product's message.

Blending—Not Brute Force

The world of branding has, for the last 50 years, relied on the brute force of repeated exposure of marketing messages to build brands.

However, the strength of a brand impression in a customer's mind is built not through powerful messages but by messages that harmonize in the customer's brain.

> ## *What does it 'sound' like to be your customer?*

The power of any one message matters only to the extent that it contributes to the blend. For example, imagine a wonderfully compelling ad that catches your attention but doesn't blend well with every other experience you have of that product. As far as you're concerned, the ad's message is very ineffective.

Brand Harmony encourages you to ask: **What does it 'sound' like to be our customer?** When interacting with you, do your customers perceive a well-integrated, cumulatively meaningful set of mutually reinforcing experiences? Or is the experience of being your customer a series of disjointed, unrelated messages that don't add up to anything understandable or relevant?

Brand Harmony Unfolds Over Time

Brand Harmony also recognizes that the 'sounds' our customers perceive—the experiences and interactions by which they evaluate our products—don't happen all at one time. It's much more like an epic symphony than a single chord. Brand impressions are cumulative running tallies that evolve through time as the customer's relationship with the product develops, where each new experience a customer has with a product gets added to the harmonic mix, helping the brand impression evolve, for better or worse. In much the same way that a stock price varies with each new piece of information, for a brand impression all news is...news.

We have discussed how strong connections between product experiences create Brand Harmony, which in turn strengthens brand impressions and encourages customers to act. How does an experience of dissonance—the discord between different product experiences—affect a customer's brand impression? In 1957, Stanford University Psychologist Leon Festinger published a paper titled "A Theory of Cognitive Dissonance," to describe the reac-

tions people have to elements of knowledge, which he calls cognitions, that are inconsistent with each other. Festinger says that
people find dissonance uncomfortable, and have a strong, innate
need to reduce it. In the case of the orchestra concert, that might
mean leaving at intermission. With a product, it may mean not
buying it anymore.

To understand the way Festinger's theory of cognitive dissonance sheds light on how customers react to product experiences,
imagine that you meet a new person and, over the first few weeks
of your acquaintance, you
grow to like this person and
find yourself pursuing a friendship. Then one day, after
you've known him for a couple
of weeks, he utters an ugly,

> *Dissonance:*
> *We feel the need to*
> *get away from it.*

hateful racist slur. You find the comment terribly offensive, and it
conflicts with the impression you'd formed of him up to this point.
Festinger says you have a strong need to reduce the dissonance
between these thoughts, which you can do by altering the importance of one of the cognitions ("Oh, he was just joking…he probably really doesn't think that way"), or by backing away from the
friendship.

A classic episode of *Seinfeld* showed how cognitive dissonance
can affect a person's brand impressions of a product. Jerry was
standing at the sink in the men's room of his favorite restaurant,
when he heard a toilet flush. The chef emerged from the stall,
chatted with Jerry for a minute, and then left the bathroom
without washing his hands. Jerry could have decided that this
wasn't an important factor ("Well, I'm sure he's planning to
wash his hands before he garnishes my entrée"), or, much more
in character, he could find himself disgusted by the situation,
ready to stop eating at the restaurant. Dissonance can drive us
away from things.

So is the key to creating Brand Harmony as simple as avoiding
brand dissonance? No. Great branding is much more than simply
not offending our customers. We have to aim much higher.

Let's look at four successive levels that move us from brand dissonance to brand harmony:

Continuum of Strength of Brand Impressions

Brand Dissonance	Brand Irrelevance	Brand Consonance	Brand Harmony

⟶

Brand Strength

1. **Brand dissonance,** which we have just discussed, describes how customers react to conflicting messages: they feel a strong, innate need to reduce the dissonance. (The ads say "we put customers first," and the sales clerk ignores you. You think, "I'll shop elsewhere.")

2. The next level is **brand irrelevance**...various messages don't conflict, but they have nothing to do with each other. (The ads say "we listen," and the sales clerk just smiles. There is no cumulative story, so the product doesn't register on your mental radar.)

3. **Brand consonance** is a situation where messages blend together, but they don't say anything compelling. (The hotel front desk clerk smiles, and the bellman says, "Have a nice day." There is a cumulative story, but it isn't very interesting. You barely notice.)

4. **Brand Harmony** describes when different product experiences blend to create a rich, interesting harmony in your mind. (The ads, brochures, interactions with salespeople, experiences of using the product and all other encounters with the product or messages about it blend to form a rich, compelling, multi-faceted story. You think, "I get it. I totally understand why I want to be involved with this product. This works for me.")

What does this continuum, from brand dissonance to Brand Harmony, tell us?

Some very important things.

Harmony is not only something greater than a lack of dissonance; it is also much greater than the mere presence of consonance. Harmony isn't about making a 'pretty' blend; it's about making a *particular* blend. The special flavor of a harmony comes from the contrast between its component parts, and the way they blend to create a special unique flavor, or character. When multiple product experiences blend to form an interesting harmony in the customer's mind, the customer can create a stronger impression of the product. Purchase decisions are not simple yes/no decisions. They are based on

> *Harmony isn't about making a 'pretty' blend; it's about combinations and contrasts that create character.*

nuance and detail that customers glean from the harmony they perceive. Rich harmony can create strong character for the product.

To illustrate this, let's look back at Ruth's decision to buy the New Beetle. What was the nature of her thoughts as she came to the conclusion to choose this car over its competitors? Were her thoughts as simple as "I like the VW and I don't like the others?" Was it that black and white?

Not at all. Ruth's thoughts about the VW were more likely along the lines of, "It's small, but it sure is cute. It doesn't drive very fast, but it handles well. I'm not crazy about the salesman, but other customers looked pretty happy with the service department guys. I love the little bud vase on the dashboard!"

Customers are willing to create rich, complex, multi-faceted thoughts about products, especially for those products that require a significant investment of money, time or emotional capital. If a customer is determining whether to become involved or stay involved with a product, he will base that decision on thoughts that have depth and detail.

Strong brand impressions have a richness of character similar to those of the most memorable literary characters. The impression that a Holden Caufield or King Lear makes on you is much more memorable than a flat, uninteresting character, because the personalities of these rich characters are so much deeper and have so many facets that you can hang on to. We want the brand impressions customers have of our products to be a lot more like Shakespeare's Sir John Falstaff—multi-faceted, complex, interesting—than Fred Flintstone—flat, monochromatic, predictable.

Richer thoughts can lead a customer to more involvement with a product. So, if you want someone to be involved with your product, you have to make it possible for him to create rich, detailed pictures of your product in his mind. Great branding is about creating an interesting, multi-part Brand Harmony in the customer's mind. Marketing efforts that try to build brand meaning with superficial, simple messages will only create superficial, simple brand impressions in customers' minds, resulting in little action and negligible loyalty.

My advertising professor in business school, Brian Sternthal, taught us that an effective ad could only carry one message. He's right. That's one of the reasons that advertising alone cannot build brands. To play a role in brand building, advertising must complement other customer interactions that can help to build rich, detailed brand impressions in a customer's mind.

Well-orchestrated brands have depth and richness. They are like personalities, in that the best of them are made interesting and beautiful by a unique blend of interesting and beautiful component parts, and the worst of them are dull and bland for lack of this blend.

Brand Harmony Implementation Step #1— What Does it Sound Like to be Your Customer?

Objective of this implementation step: To gain a quick under-standing of whether you create a harmonious or dissonant set of experiences for your customers.

Time required: 1 hour

We've been discussing how a perception of Brand Harmony influences a customer's opinion of a product. How well are you doing—right now—at creating Brand Harmony in the minds of your customers?

Take a moment and re-read the orchestra parable at the beginning of this book. Now imagine that the audience members are your customers and the concert is being presented by your company.

- What is the experience like for your customers?
- Are you telling them a clear story?
- Do the operations of your organization reinforce the promises of your advertising and promotional communications, or do they conflict, like the workman in the orchestra story?
- Does the purchase process help customers form positive brand impressions, or does it get in the way, as it does in the story?
- What about the performance of the product itself?
- What about customer service?
- What else about your product does the customer experience?

Get together with some colleagues and brainstorm these questions, taking notes on easel paper, digging into issues that seem important to you. As you do this, draw a picture on the paper of all of the inputs that reach your customer, similar to the graphic of Ruth on page 12. Which of these inputs are help-ing to strengthen Brand Harmony in your customers' minds, and which are diluting it? Which are the most critical inputs?

Be especially free-thinking and energetic in your brain-storming. Don't worry about being too exact or making any final pronouncements—there's plenty of time for that later. Use this as a chance to get a quick audit of how well you're doing creating Brand Harmony in your customers' minds.

As you work through this implementation step, summarize the current state of Brand Harmony from your customers' perspectives. How clear is the story you are telling them? Is it easy for them to 'get it' as they interact with you? How much would you like the experience of dealing with your company if you were one of your customers?

Brand Harmony Implementation Step #2—
What Do They Think of You Now?

Objective of this implementation step: Understand the current brand impressions in your customers' minds.

Time required: 3–5 days of time for an interviewer (Interviews will last 15–20 minutes. Figure on a total time of 30 minutes per interview to account for leaving phone messages, waiting on hold and writing up notes after the calls.) Then, add an additional ½ day to review the findings with the interviewer to interpret what was learned.

We've said that your brand is not what you say you are, but what your customers think you are.

So...what is your current brand? When your customers think about you, what do they think? Is it something rich and meaningful, or nondescript and vague? Is it relevant and motivating, or is it something they barely notice? Is it distinct or generic?

This implementation step is designed to give us a benchmark of the current brand impressions customers have of your product. The thoughts your customers have are the true measures of the state of your brand.

If you have a substantial market research program, you may already have a good idea of what customers think of you. Congratulations. You're one in a thousand. If, on the other hand, you're like most companies, you haven't done the research needed to answer the questions listed above. Not to worry—this implementation step will show you an easy way to get a rough idea of what's going on.

To do this, conduct one-on-one interviews with 25-50 customers of your product, and, if possible, 10 to 25 prospective customers who are familiar with your product.

- If possible, have a neutral third party who has nothing to gain or lose by the answers from customers conduct the interviews. (i.e., don't let salespeople interview their own customers!)

Start with the following open-ended question (inserting your company or product name in place of "XYZ"): **What do you think about XYZ?**

- You want to ask questions that are very open ended. You want to learn what the customer thinks, and if you ask really specific questions, you'll hear what the customer thinks you want to hear, as opposed to what she really thinks.

Probe further based on the responses the customer gives. Don't steer her to any particular topic; let her set the agenda.

Next, ask these questions as follow up:

- **What would you say to someone who asks, 'Who or what is XYZ?'**
- **What does XYZ do?**
- **What does XYZ do for you? (Or, in the case of prospective customers, "what do you think XYZ could do for you?)**

And, if possible, try to glean more general information about the customer's interests, needs, attitudes and habits related to this kind of product.

After the interview process, spend a ½ day with the interviewer to review the responses and draw some insights. What you are looking for is a glimpse into your customer's thoughts, a sneak peek into their minds. You are not looking for a statistically valid set of facts that can be placed on a matrix, so don't expect to find them! You are getting acquainted with your customers' thoughts, in the same way you get acquainted with a new friend. Look at the information the interviewer has gathered, and as you become familiar with it try to identify the trends and issues that are most significant. You should be able to summarize what you learn into a rough description of the current state of your brand.

5

Designing
Brand Harmony

Forget Your "Unique Selling Proposition." What's Your "Desired Brand Perception?"

Blending a Customer's Experiences to Create Brand Harmony

What makes one piece of music different from another? What distinguishes different food, wines or perfumes?

The character of each of these is determined by the various components they are made of and the way those components blend with each other. Stravinsky's Rite of Spring and Mozart's Jupiter Symphony are both harmonious, yet they have completely different harmonic characters. The same thing happens with food, wine, perfumes or many other things that enter our senses. You may love two marinara sauces, yet they can both taste completely different. Each has its own flavor.

The art of the composer, chef, vintner or perfume designer is in the way they blend different components together to form a particular harmony or special character. Our task is similar as we create Brand Harmony. Our branding palette includes the entire set of experiences customers have with our products, and our art is to *orchestrate* those customers' experiences into a harmony that evokes certain rich, complex thoughts—or brand impressions—in those who perceive it.

Brand Harmony that is artfully orchestrated encourages customers to be more involved with a product. Its value is more than aesthetic; great Brand Harmony is motivational. The orchestration of Brand Harmony is far from random. It is designed with the specific task of persuading customers to do things that help a product reach its performance goals.

This chapter will address the process of designing Brand Harmony. We will discuss how to blend product experiences in a way that creates a particular character for the brand, but we will do it with keen focus on the business results our brand strategy is trying to create.

To begin our discussion of creating Brand Harmony, let's return to this model (Figure 6), which we first saw in Chapter 2. Since it demonstrates the direct connection between every experience the customer has with your product and the product's ultimate success, we call it "The Brand Harmony Results Model."

The Brand Harmony Results Model is our road map to creating a successful program of Brand Harmony, and this chapter will show you how to apply it to your business. We will work through

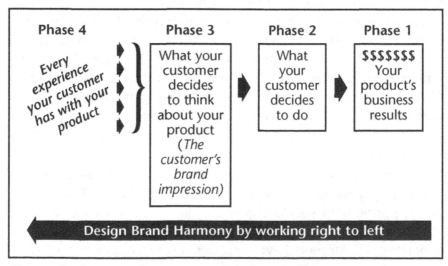

Figure 6. **The Brand Harmony Results Model**

the model from right to left, starting with a focus on the business results that you want to achieve for your product. The reason for this can be found in an old saying: "If you don't know where you're going, any road will lead you there." By defining the destination of our journey before we begin, we will be able to make much better decisions at every phase of the process.

As we work through the Brand Harmony Results Model from right to left, we will answer the following questions in four successive phases:

Phase 1: How do we define success for our product?

Phase 2: What customer action will help us reach that success? Who are the customers that we are talking about?

Phase 3: What thoughts in the minds of customers will be most likely to encourage customers to do the things we want them to do?

Phase 4: What orchestrated set of product experiences are most likely to encourage customers to think the thoughts we'd like them to think?

Brand Harmony describes a process through which your customers evaluate you by scrutinizing every interaction they have with your organization. Your efforts to design Brand Harmony must be grounded in a thorough understanding of the way your organization and its products interact with customers and your environment.

Let's explore how to use the Brand Harmony Results Model to improve the quality of your customers' Brand Harmony experience by starting at the far right box, "Your Product's Business Results."

PHASE 1 FOR DESIGNING BRAND HARMONY: *CREATING A PICTURE OF SUCCESS*

Success is not a generic term. Successful marketing is not just about 'selling more stuff.' Success comes in many flavors, and the particular kind of success you are striving for has an influence on every marketing decision you make.

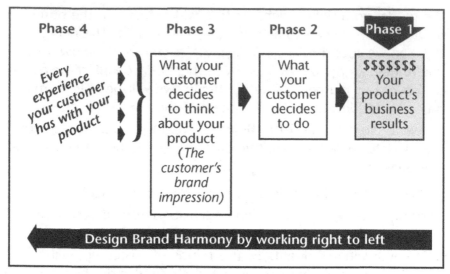

Figure 7. **The Brand Harmony Results Model**

Most branding and marketing communications efforts don't have clearly defined business objectives, other than weak proxies such as 'raising awareness.' This makes it difficult to create focused, effective marketing plans. It is important to create a detailed, relevant and descriptive *picture of success* for your marketing and branding efforts—before you start them.

This picture of success can not be fabricated from the imagination. It needs to be based on a realistic understanding of the world in which your product lives. You need to start by refining this understanding so that you can identify the most important and relevant goals for your branding program. You want to be able to answer questions such as, "What's going on in our world? Why is it happening? Why does it matter?"

Answering these questions will help you discover the most critical issues that affect your product's results. Discovering these issues will help you create your picture of success.

Thousands of techniques for business analysis, competitive analysis, customer research and strategic planning exist, and the methods your organization currently uses may be entirely appropriate for this process. Our goal at this stage of the process is to discuss how the methods you currently use, along with methods introduced here, can be integrated into the process of creating a strong experience of Brand Harmony for your customers. If, on the other hand, your organization does not employ many analysis and planning tools, the ideas presented here are a good place to start.

Whatever business analysis methods you use, however, it is important at this stage of the process to free yourself from any preconceived notions of what the most important issues are which affect your business. Many people, at this point, are tempted to sit down and quickly make a list of the most important issues that affect their situation. The problem with this is that the issues that are top of mind today may not be the most important long term issues. The bigger chal-

"Top of mind" business issues may not be the most important issues

lenge is to uncover issues lurking beneath the surface that you may not have been thinking about. I call this process "panning for gold," because it can help you bring these hidden issues to the surface so that you can consider them along with the more conspicuous issues facing your business. The key to this process is to ask lots of questions about your business without jumping to any quick conclusions that discount ideas before they are explored. Like a prospector sifting his pan in a mountain stream, as you explore these issues the most valuable will glisten and sparkle, revealing themselves as special and important.

Every issue you need to consider will fall into one of the following four categories:

1. Your customers
2. Your competitors
3. The market environment
4. Your organization

Issues from these four categories serve as the fuel for your branding and business strategy process. The better you understand which of these issues most affect your business, the more effective your branding process will be.

Let's explore each of these categories of issues.

Customer Issues that Impact Your Picture of Success

The kinds of questions you might want to ask about customers include:

- Who are they?
- Who could they be?
- What do they care about?
- What do they think about us and our product?
- How do they behave?

One of the most prevalent, chronic maladies of modern business is an inadequate understanding of customers. Try asking a group of senior executives from a company to describe their customers, and what you will likely hear is a set of inconsistent answers, some meaningless demographic platitudes, or both. Companies don't know enough about who their customers are, why they buy, who else they buy from and, frequently, how much they buy. I have often seen companies claiming to be customer focused without a shared understanding of customers throughout the organization at anything more than a simplistic, superficial level.

In an article in the 1998-1999 issue of Northwestern University's Medill School's *Journal of Integrated Marketing Communications,* Dr. Lisa Fortini-Campbell contrasts this simplistic way of looking at customers with the assiduous efforts actors employ to get to know their characters. Actors tenaciously probe every facet of their characters' personalities and motivations, getting to know their characters so well that they actually "become" those characters. It is common practice for actors, as a way to get better acquainted with their characters, to look beyond the available information in the script and try to imagine how their characters would react in different life situations. Marketers, on the other hand, are too quick to jump to conclusions about their customers, and are too quick to lump them into faceless, homogenous categories. If actors had such broad, ill-defined views of their characters, their performances would get panned.

Brute force branding, with its heavy reliance on media advertising and large-scale direct marketing, inherently relies on broad, generalized groupings of customers. Advertising is forced to use prospective customers' media habits as proxies for purchase behaviors, and direct mail programs often do a similar thing by creating models and profiles of customers to predict what they will buy. These methods can be effective at creating sales, but use of these techniques over the years has caused many people to confuse these proxies with the actual customers they are trying to describe. Often times if you ask someone, "Who is your customer?" you get a response such as "$65,000 income, female with 2.7 kids, own their own home."

Demographics sound smart and authoritative, so they are often quoted. The problem is that they are often very misleading. Obviously, statistics like those described above represent just an average customer. And because of that, they can be very dangerous. In a marketplace such as ours that has come to recognize increased variation and individuality of customers, focus on a theoretical, average customer has clear dangers. Inherent in a customer population of increased variation is that an individual customer looks much less like the average customer than in a more homogenous population. Marketing to the average will therefore ensure that the marketing message is irrelevant to most customers.

I was once asked to help a mid-level manager at an advertising agency on a marketing plan for one of her client's products. The target audience for the product was anyone who uses an ATM machine, which, at that time, was about 50% of the American public in any given month. She insisted that her target customer was a household with an income of $50,000, headed by someone 18–34 years of age, a fact that was based on a statistic she had picked up describing the average ATM customer. She wanted to use this demographic fact as a foundation for her marketing efforts, and she had already decided that she should use radio advertising targeted at people who fit this demographic description. I explained to her that since the use of ATMs was so broad and that since this was just an *average* number, focusing advertising on this fictitious average customer would ensure that she would *not* be marketing to most of her target customers. She looked at me blankly, with no idea what I was talking about.

It is important to avoid the temptation to group your customers into sets that make it easier for you to think about them but don't truly describe them. Demographics and other descriptions of customer characteristics only matter to you at this point if they help you understand customer behavior and buying characteristics. At this point in the process you are trying to get better acquainted with your customers and the issues that affect their involvement with your product, and these proxies can obscure the important issues you are trying to uncover.

Other signs can reveal that a company is not truly focused on its customers. Where does management spend its time? Compare the amount of time senior execs spend dealing with customer issues to the amount of time they spend on budgets, compensation issues, corporate finance, office politics and allocations of office space. Compare the amount of time marketing department staffers spend dealing with customer issues with the time they spend focusing on budgets, production schedules, turf wars and bemoaning the meddling of senior management in their lives. How often do executives and managers actually talk with real, live customers? How frequently does the executive with more political power get his way, the customers' best interests notwithstanding? Is employee compensation based on meeting customer needs? What is the ratio of money spent talking at customers vs. money spent listening to customers?

Gaining an understanding of customers that is shared throughout an organization is a long-term, ongoing process that requires a significant commitment from an organization. Just because an organization launches a 'voice of the customer' initiative and professes a customer focus does not guarantee that it will be in touch with its customers.

Creating a Culture of Curiosity About Customers

As the Brand Harmony Results Model shows, customer attitudes and action have everything to do with an organization's success. One of the healthiest things a company can do to improve its results is become more in touch with its customers—who they are, who they could be, what they care about, how they behave and how they think about the company and its products.

This doesn't mean that you ask customers what they want and reflexively grant their wishes. It means that you have a clear understanding of what they do and don't want so you can focus your scarce resources on things that count. It means that you understand your customers so well that you can anticipate what they would want in situations that they have not yet thought of. It means that you develop a "culture of curiosity" where everyone in the company becomes a passionate, engaged, enthusiastic student of the customer.

This book is not meant to be a treatise on market research; there are plenty of other sources for that information. Our purpose here is to outline the kinds of customer information that can help you develop a brand strategy, and you can integrate these ideas with any of the market research tools you use, no matter how extensive or limited they may be. Whatever methods for customer inquiry that you choose, constantly asking your customers questions and observing what they do is imperative to gain the understanding you need for effective branding.

Never Stop Asking Your Customers Questions

Many small companies avoid market research because it is too expensive and too technical. Many large companies invest in formal market research, but then don't do much else to understand their customers. Neither scenario is healthy.

Formal market research is great; if you can afford it, do it and do it often. However, it is not the only way to ask questions of customers. If your budgets don't allow for professional market research studies, you can still put in place a more informal practice of customer interviews and round table discussions. Here are some things to think about if you try this:

- If possible, use an objective interviewer or moderator from outside the company who has some basic familiarity with your industry. This is much less expensive than commissioning a formal market research study and it will keep bias to a minimum.
- Ask open ended questions. Make a very general query, and then be quiet. Let the customer talk; you'll be able to tell what is important to her by the subjects she chooses to talk about.
- Do interviews and round table discussions on a regular basis. You'll know you're doing it frequently enough when you start to be able to predict what you're going to hear.
- Don't expect customers to give you all the answers. They may not be able to articulate exactly what they want, but you can gain insights into how they think and what they care about. Qualitative research isn't designed to provide definitive answers. It's designed to make you smarter about your customers.
- Don't "mix and match" participants in round table discussions. People are most honest and forthright when they are in the company of peers, in addition to being more likely to engage in spirited debate. Talk to employees separately from their supervisors, group similar kinds of customers together, etc.

Pay special attention to the question *"what do your customers think about you and your product?"* One of the central principles of Brand Harmony is that "your brand is not what you say you are, but what your customer thinks you are." What customers currently think of your product represents the current state of your brand. For this reason, it is important to get a benchmark of what customers think of you now.

Never Stop Observing What Your Customers Do

Jerry Hirschberg, president of Nissan Design, tells a great story[6] about how his team determined the best colors for a line of children's furniture. The tendency, of course, is for adults to think that kids want things in big, bold primary colors. While observing children at play in a day care center, one of Jerry's designers got down on the floor and asked one of the children if she could see his box of crayons. She poured the crayons out and looked for those that were the shortest, i.e., the most used. Those colors did not happen to be the bold, primary colors that most would have guessed they would be. The result was a line of children's furniture in earth tones. Most of your customers aren't as forthcoming and honest as children; they may not tell you their favorite color, but you certainly can look for their shortest crayons.

Customer behavior is one of the most telling truths in business, and one of the best ways to learn about your customers is to watch them and listen to them. Your sales statistics are a treasure trove of customer insights. Break numbers apart, and look for nuggets of gold in their components One of the most basic aspects of business hygiene is being fluent with customer sales data, but I can't tell you how often I see companies for whom this kind of information is hidden.

Put in place means to observe your customers while they are in the process of interacting with your organization and your product. Can you set up 'observation posts' throughout your series of customer touch-points, where customer attitudes and actions can be recorded for appropriate feedback For example, if your business is a retail store, is there a mechanism in place that transmits relevant customer comments from the point of sale to appropriate decision makers? Which competitors' shopping bags are customers carrying when they enter the store? If they don't buy, how much time do they spend in the store before they leave? What kinds of questions do they ask?

Managers at Ikea regularly follow customers through their furniture stores, watching where they go and how they behave. They noted that men weren't following their wives into the textile department, so they set up a display of tools at the entrance to that department. They claim that this move helped them sell a lot of screwdrivers.[7]

Involve your entire organization in this culture of customer curiosity. Wouldn't you be happy if a front line employee ran up to a senior person in your company and said, excitedly, "I just learned the coolest thing about a customer today!" Would that be likely to happen in your organization? Why couldn't it?

Competitive Issues that Impact Your Picture of Success

The kinds of competitive questions you want to ask are:

- Who are your competitors?
- Who could they be?
- What are your strengths and weaknesses relative to them?
- What opportunities and threats do these strengths and weaknesses imply?

Far and away, the most common mistake made in competitive analysis is believing that a company gets to define its own competitive set. A competitive set is not defined by a company, but by its customers; if another product is a viable option for your customers, it is your competitor. Hotel executives are notorious for making this mistake. A resort general manager in a vacation destination once tried to persuade me that the hotel next to his wasn't a competitor because they had prices significantly lower than his. As he saw it, his competitive set included only the other resorts that priced at a level similar to his, and he looked superciliously at any of his neighbor hotels that had "cheapened" themselves. Unfortunately, his customers saw it differently.

This mistake does not only result in ignoring competitors. Sometimes it causes companies to pay too much attention to competitors who are not even on their customers' radar screens. You may see a competitor as a rival, but gauge your reactions to their moves based on how your customers see them, not as you see them.

Another common mistake is not understanding your competitors' strategies. The marketing department of a large national advertiser was able to show me detailed reports of every television commercial their competitors ran, but they could not tell me what the brand strategy was in those commercials. This kind of myopia encourages ad hoc, tactical competitive reactions, and makes it unlikely that a company can craft a strategic approach to dealing with its competitors.

Issues from the Market Environment that Impact Your Picture of Success

The main question you need to ask here is:

- What factors from our external environment, which are outside of our control, affect us?

It may be the weather, it may be terrorism, it may be the economy...there are many issues over which we have no control that influence our business results. Do you run a restaurant in an urban neighborhood that is going through gentrification? This may offer you an opportunity to command higher prices and attract a more affluent clientele, suggesting a change in your brand strategy. Are you considering a national roll out of a product at time when California is introducing legislation that could affect your ability to sell there? This may suggest that you rethink your national strategy and not waste efforts in California.

New legislation always sends lawyers, accountants and financial planners scurrying to find new opportunities to serve their clients. Changes in estate tax rates prompt life insurance sales people to change the focus of their sales pitches. Changes in the cost of living index influence the way unions sell their latest wage increase proposals to management. You can't stop the waves, but you sure can surf them!

The aftermath of the terror attacks on September 11, 2001 caused many businesses to rethink their marketing and brand strategies. Vacation destinations like The Cayman Islands emphasized that they were among the safest islands in the Caribbean, while the U.S. Virgin Islands advertised their tie to America. MSNBC became "America's News Channel" and Paula Zahn decided that her personal brand could not afford to miss the action, so she took the anchor chair at CNN many months before her contract required her to. Many businesses reacted to the tough economic climate by lowering prices and promoting themselves for the first time as a low cost alternative...a brand-diluting move that many of them now regret.

There are many factors affecting your product over which you have no control. You may not be able to change these factors, but a thorough understanding of them can help you navigate through your environment as you define a winning brand strategy.

Issues from Your Organization that Impact Your Picture of Success

This category of issues helps you answer the question:

- What about you and your organization—its interests, goals, financial dynamic, people, organization structure, ownership structure, strengths, weaknesses, etc.—will affect strategy?

An honest, introspective assessment of your organization is critical to developing a brand strategy. You don't want to communicate a brand promise that requires your organization to do things it is not good at. Conversely, you don't want to miss the opportunity to base a brand strategy on things that your organization excels at.

Most importantly, as we try to create a picture of success for your products, it is critical to consider issues related to the organization's goals and the dynamics of how it produces results. Are you a public company that needs to produce impressive quarterly results, or is yours a family business most interested in developing long-term value for subsequent generations? This can say a lot about the kind of customer behavior you want to encourage, and about the brand impressions that will drive that behavior. Does the profitability of a customer increase at an increasing rate as that customer's purchase volume increases? Or is yours a product for which transaction costs are low and you make no more money off a single transaction with a big customer than you do from a single transaction with a small customer? These two scenarios might lead you to two completely different brand strategies. Is your product one for which add-on products produce disproportionate profits, such as a movie theater's sales of snacks or a car rental company's upgrades to larger cars? If so, you'll want to consider that factor as you develop your strategy.

Your company's organization structure will also say a lot about the kind of brand impressions it is capable of creating in customers' minds. Do your sales people have strong technical skills related to your product? Are you understaffed in front line positions? Do you offer 24/7 customer service?

Understanding these kinds of issues about your organization will help you create a brand strategy that you can live up to...and one that you will want to live up to.

Translating What You Learn into a Picture of Success

In order to prepare to create a picture of success for your products, we have been exploring issues related to your customers, your competitors, the market environment and your organization. Here is a sampling of the kinds of issues different businesses might uncover:

- Samples of important customer issues—
  - The share of your business which comes from your top 5 customers has dropped significantly in the past year.
  - You are losing customers in the American Southwest but gaining them in New England.
  - 68% of your business comes from single parent homes.
  - You don't know very much about who your individual customers are.
- Samples of important competitive issues—
  - Prospective customers continually confuse you with a major competitor.
  - Your closest competitor has just launched an effort to steal your biggest customers.
- Samples of important market environment issues—

- There is major legislation pending in congress that would give customers a tax break for purchasing your product.
- Rising interest rates could make it hard for your customers to make capital investments, presenting an opportunity to sell long term maintenance contracts.
- The El Nino weather pattern could affect your suppliers' ability to grow crops you needs as key ingredients for your product.

- Samples of important issues related to your organization—
  - Marketing costs now exceed 15% of sales for your largest selling product. It's historically been 8%.
  - Your sales people each have a favorite product to sell, pushing that product to the exclusion of others.
  - Your owners have decided to take a long term view, encouraging you to invest in finding new products for new markets.

There is no 'right' number of key issues for you to identify, although any more than eight is difficult to deal with. Ideally, you will be able to focus your list down to three or four key factors that will drive your branding decisions. Your particular list of key issues may be focused largely on customer issues, with no key issues related to the competition. Or, conversely, you find that competitive issues are the most important issues you face. After September 11, 2001 many companies found the most important issues confronting them to be market environment issues—those over which they have no control.

As you focus in on these key issues, look for ways to translate them into performance objectives that can be part of your emerging picture of success. To use some of the examples from above:

- If 68% of your business is now from single parent homes, is this is a sign that you could grow this business even further next year, enabling you to set a lofty goal for sales to this market segment?
- If revenues from your largest customers are shrinking, do you need to set objectives related to repeat purchases and

account penetration? And/or does this situation suggest a need to set objectives related to new customer acquisition?

- If your largest competitor is going after your most important customers, do you need to set quantifiable, measurable objectives related to retaining that business?
- If the weather will restrict your availability to sources of supply for certain products, should you change your forecasted product sales mix to reflect this?
- If your sales people are focusing on single product sales, should you redefine sales success in terms of account penetration (share of customer) instead of product volume (share of market)?

Your picture of success should be a detailed, clear vision of where you want to be and what success means to you. Be willing to dig deep. Your picture of success may have many components and sub-objectives, each of them related to key issues that you identified while 'panning for gold'. Don't look for one, grandiose objective, such as "be the preferred supplier in our marketplace." Objectives like that are so vague that it is impossible to decide what to do next. Instead, define a series of tangible, understandable and relevant business goals that are narrow enough to suggest clear action in our subsequent phases.

Pitfalls to Avoid in Phase 1 of Designing Brand Harmony

Before you start working on the implementation steps that follow, consider some of the things that can go wrong as you try to 'pan for gold' and create a picture of success:

- **Saying "no" too soon**

    Many issues will come up in the panning for gold process. There will often be a tendency to say, "Oh, we'll never be able to do that," or "Are you kidding? Our CEO would never agree to that!" Avoid those reactions. You want to find the real issues, not just those that are politically acceptable. At this stage in the process, don't discount ideas just because they seem difficult to address. You will have plenty of opportunities to filter ideas later.

- **Letting pre-conceived ideas about your business obscure the real issues that arise**

  Be willing to question all of your current assumptions about your customers, your competitors, your market environment and your own organization. Beware of long term biases held by your organization. The process of panning for gold may suggest a need to change course and recast your business objectives. Ignoring this information can be like ignoring driving directions. You may end up stuck at the end of a cul de sac.

- **Don't guess**

  Hypotheses and intuition are good, because they are based on underlying information and ideas. But blind guesses can be deadly.

- **Defining objectives too broadly**

  Broad objectives, such as "Increase sales by $2 million," are hard to act on. When presented with a goal like this, your first question is, "Ok, what do I do now?" Breaking these wide-ranging goals down into smaller, component objectives will make it easier to create strategies and action plans in subsequent phases of this process.

- **Defining small objectives that don't contribute to broader objectives.**

  Smaller objectives can be acted on, but it's important that they eventually contribute to your overall goals. Efforts to achieve objectives require scarce resources, so be careful not to get distracted by peripheral, non-essential goals. Every small success should fit into the larger picture of helping you reach your overall goals.

- **Confusing business objectives with brand perceptions**

  I can't begin to count the number of times I have seen companies say they have an objective to be the "preferred supplier in the marketplace." This is not a business objective. Business objectives describe business outcomes, not the customer perceptions that help you achieve those objectives.

Brand Harmony Implementation Step #3— Panning for Gold

Objective of this implementation step: *To identify the most critical issues driving your strategy, preparing you to create a picture of success.*

Time required:
- Preparation phase: *varies, depending on the accessibility and scope of available information*
- Brainstorming phase: *4–6 hours*

This is a critical step for developing a brand strategy based on Brand Harmony. It is where you ask, "What's really going on, and why?" It will help you filter through the many issues which affect your business to find those that are most important to your success.

As described in the text above, every issue that can affect your brand strategy falls into one of the following four categories:

1. Your customers: *For example: Who are they? Who could they be? What do they care about? How do they behave? What do they think about you and your product? Etc....*
2. Your competitors: *What are your strengths and weaknesses relative to them, and what opportunities and threats do these imply?*
3. You market environment: *What factors from your external environment, which are outside of your control, affect you?*
4. Your organization: *What about you and your organization— its interests, goals, financial dynamics, people, organization structure, ownership structure, strengths, weaknesses, etc.— will affect strategy?*

In this implementation step we will sort through these kinds of issues, panning for gold to allow the most important ones to reveal themselves. The implementation step falls into two phases, a preparation phase and a brainstorming phase. In the preparation phase you will gather information related to the four issue categories listed above that can be used in your brainstorming session.

Panning for Gold: Preparation and Information Gathering Phase

Look at the questions posed above for each of the four issue categories. Assemble as much information as you can that can help you answer these questions. Here are the kinds of data that can help you in your brainstorming session:

- Customers
  - The results of the implementation steps at the end of chapter 4 can help you understand customers' current perceptions and experiences with your company and its products.
  - Customer sales data—who your customers are, sorted by as many different variables as possible: size of customer, industry, geography, purchase volume, changes in purchase volume, products purchased, channels they purchase through, etc. Slice and dice the information in lots of different ways—you never know what patterns you may discover. If possible, estimate what share of each customer's business for your type of product goes to you.
  - Any research data that can help you understand customers' interests and needs—
    · Secondary research: can you purchase any research from industry sources?
    · Primary research: you may have learned some valuable lessons in Implementation Step #2. If you think you're still in the dark on these issues, you may want to do some more interviews or roundtable discussions to probe further.
- Competitors
  - One of the quickest ways to gather information about your competitors is to ask some of your customers to give you their perspective. They can tell you who they think your competitors are and what their strengths and weak-

nesses are relative to you. Remember: a competitor is only a competitor if your customers think it is a competitor.

- Other good sources for competitive information include people who work for trade magazines or trade associations, and salespeople who have been around the industry for many years.

• The market environment
- Update your knowledge of forecasts and trends related to factors that are out of your control but affect your business. For example, if you're an airline or a taxi service, you might want to do some quick research on trends in fuel prices. If you run a labor intensive business, you may want to get the most current unemployment data. If you run a corner cafe you may want to understand trends in new home construction in your community.

• Your organization
- Gather together performance data that might shed light on important issues: sales and profitability data broken down by product, industry segment, channel, geography, seasonality, etc.
- Metrics typically measured by businesses in your industry can be valuable: Examples could include revenue per employee, direct product cost as a percentage of revenue, etc.

Panning for Gold: Brainstorming Phase

Block out 4 hours to dig into these issues with your Brand Harmony brainstorming colleagues. Bring the information you gathered in the preparation and information gathering phase, in order to help you answer the questions above. Using the questions on page 63 as your guide, explore the four issue categories: your customers, your competitors, the market environment and your organization.

Designate one person as facilitator, with plenty of easel paper handy, and dig in!

- Don't be linear! There is no special order to answering these questions, and, if you're doing it right, you will be tempted to jump from issue to issue as your ideas start to percolate. That's ok...if you're not ready to talk about it when it comes up, write it on a piece of easel paper, stick it to the wall and then draw a big blue arrow pointing to it, so you won't forget to come back to it later.

- Err on the side of having too many ideas. Don't filter too early. Accumulate ideas and insights, look for connections, and explore with the curiosity of a toddler who has just discovered the cabinet with pots and pans.

- Make note of what you don't know. You will inevitably come across questions that you are not equipped to answer. That's to be expected; keep track of what you don't know, and as you focus in on critical issues you'll be able to define what additional information gathering steps are worth taking.

Pan for Gold!

- As you go through this process, certain ideas and issues will naturally show themselves to be more important and valuable than the rest. Like nuggets of gold shining through the muck and mud of a prospector's pan, these issues will beg for you to extract them. Look at them from all angles, and then polish them to reveal all of their worth.

- Use the brightest marker you have to circle these issues as they become evident.

- Begin a list of these key issues—the nuggets of gold—on a new piece of easel paper once you have identified four of them.

- If the list expands beyond eight, start trying to consolidate the issues. It's hard to factor more than eight issues into your brand strategy; in fact, you're lucky if you find 3-4 that are much more important than the rest. This will make it much easier for you to focus your branding efforts.

Brand Harmony Implementation Step #4— Creating a Picture of Success

Objective of this implementation step: Define, in a way that is meaningful and specific, what success you hope to achieve from your branding efforts.

Time required: ½–1 day to identify the list of objectives you want to achieve. The time required for defining the specific quantifiable aspects of these objectives will vary depending on the nature of the objectives and your organization's forecasting process.

"If you don't know where you're going, any road will lead you there." It's surprising how many marketing programs waste effort on ill-defined goals. This implementation step will help you avoid that problem by answering the question, "Where do we want to be?"

Your panning for gold process in the previous implementation step identified a number of key issues that your strategy must address. These represent issues and forces that can have a great impact on your success or failure, because so much rests on what happens in regard to them.

Your current challenge is to translate these important issues into performance objectives. Refer back to pages 60–61 for some examples of how this works. Essentially, you are determining what would happen to your business if you could either neutralize a negative issue or capitalize on a positive issue. At the end of this implementation step you should have a list of business outcomes that are quantifiable in terms of time and money, or, if money isn't your objective, some other tangible measure of performance. (An example of a non-monetary measure of performance: you are trying to persuade homeless people to use your soup kitchen, and you measure success by the number of meals you give away.)

You may define more than one measure of success for each key issue. For example, if you identified waning customer loyalty as a key issue when panning for gold, you may define a number of measures of increased loyalty, e.g., reduced customer attrition, more transactions per customer per year, more revenue per customer per year, more products purchased by each customer, etc.

The challenge is to identify performance objectives that are specific enough for action, but broad enough to merit attention. For example, a non-specific objective like "increase customer retention" is admirable as a starting point, but it leaves you asking, "What do I do to get started?" This broad objective needs to be broken down into narrower, more manageable objectives, such as "increase annual retention of national account customers to 95% within 2 years." Recognize that big objectives are the sum of smaller objectives. Understand where you want to be, on a comprehensive level, and what smaller, component objectives will help you get there.

One trick to make this process easier is to separate it into two phases:

- In the first phase, create a list of the objectives you wish to achieve, with only a general description of what you want to happen. For example, you may be able to identify quickly that you want to declare an objective of increasing customer retention among a certain group of customers.

- In the second phase, fine tune the quantifiable aspects of these objectives. For example, it may take a little longer to define exactly which customers you want to retain and what specific retention rates are most appropriate.

By breaking this process into these two phases you'll be able to move ahead quickly without getting bogged down in details that can be addressed at a later time.

When you are done with this process, you should be able to list the key performance measures for your efforts. In other words, you will have created a picture of success.

PHASE 2 FOR DESIGNING BRAND HARMONY:
DEFINING THE CUSTOMER ACTION YOU NEED TO HELP YOU ACHIEVE SUCCESS

The previous phase set the stage for exploring the next box in our model—what we want customers to do to help us reach success.

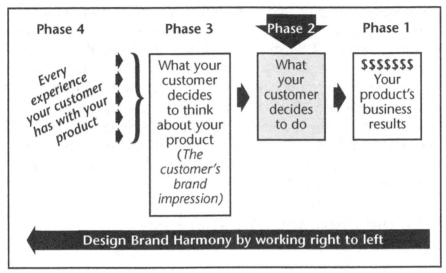

Figure 8. **The Brand Harmony Results Model**

There are many ways to improve a product's bottom line. There may be opportunities on the cost side, such as negotiating lower prices from suppliers, and there may be opportunities on the revenue side by encouraging different behavior from customers.

Although opportunities to cut costs exist in every organization, most organizations I see have already gone through many rounds of cost cutting, and the incremental remaining benefit to most organizations from cutting costs pales next to the opportunities that are still available to them on the revenue side. In other words, for most

The connection between customer action and business results

organizations, the greatest potential for increased profitability will be realized by getting more from customers, not by spending less on suppliers. "Getting more from customers" happens when customers behave in a way that improves your results. This could happen when they become customers, become better customers, refer their friends, etc.

The connection between customer action and results is true even if you do not define success purely in financial terms. If you run a youth literacy program and have defined success in terms of 'books read per student,' it is more likely that the actions of your customers—students—have more impact on your success than whether you are able to negotiate a 5% discount on your rent. Customer action is the key driver of improved success for most products.

My personal definition of marketing is "persuading customers to do things that help you reach your particular vision of success." The goal of this phase is to identify specifically who those customers are and what it is we want them to do to help make your picture of success a reality.

Who the Customers Are that Help You Reach Success

Consider the picture of success you have created. What do these insights tell you about which customer groups are important to your success? Does the picture suggest a focus on customers in certain geographic regions? A focus on customers in certain demographic or industry segments? Are portions of your current customer base more critical than others in helping you reach your goals? What kinds of prospective new customers would be most important to you?

As we discussed above in Phase 1, it is important to avoid grouping customers into sets that don't describe their actual purchase interests or behavior, such as defining customers by their television watching habits. Media usage can describe how to reach a customer with advertising, but it doesn't help you understand if a certain type of customer can help you reach your business goals. Another example of a customer grouping that can be misleading is the way many companies assign customers to salespeople geographically. As with advertising, where media usage forms a convenient proxy for grouping customers, geographical allocation of customers to salespeople is a convenient way for a company to organize its customers. It reflects the company's organization chart, but it may not reflect the way customers make purchase decisions.

Unfortunately, people have a tendency to confuse these groupings of customers, which are done for the convenience of marketing and sales people, with the actual *characteristics* of customers. At this point in the process, you should not be thinking about how you reach customers, through advertising, sales or any other means. That comes later. Now you are trying to identify which customers can help you reach your goals, and it is important that you jettison any preconceived notions about your customers that might obstruct the answers you are looking for.

Another problem with identifying customers happens in companies that are organized into product management groups. Managers in charge of certain products tend to understand customers only in terms of the sales experience their particular product has had with those customers. When trying to identify the customers that can help them meet their goals, these companies often miss opportunities that could be revealed by a better understanding of how customers relate to other parts of their organization. For example, lawyers tend to have specialties, and a law firm may have certain partners focused on areas such as commercial litigation and others focused on providing real estate legal services to the same types of clients. These lawyers often miss opportunities to sell their own services to their partners' clients, for the simple reason that each of them has an independent view of the client that is not coordinated with everyone else's. Like the parable of the five blind men describing an elephant based only on the part they touch, each attorney sees the client only from his own perspective. This is a common problem in companies that sell business-to-business products, severely limiting the company's ability to cross-sell its products to customers. The company is organized according to the way they produce their products, and there is no one who looks at the whole potential of the customer. The result: a missed opportunity to cross-sell products.

Another challenge involves *decision influencers,* the people who influence purchase decisions made by others. For example, you're selling to a purchasing manager, but his decision needs to be approved by the vice-president of engineering. The problem: you've never met the vice-president of engineering.

Decision influencers are often elusive, and frequently critical to your success. One of the most common examples of decision influencers is the child who has no money to her own name, but the power to induce mom and dad to make certain purchases. The world of marketing learned to understand the decision-influencing power of kids long ago. However, the power of decision influencers in the business-to-business marketplace presents challenges that many organizations still struggle with. Frequently a company will have a main point of contact within a client organization, with no direct access to others who can influence purchase decisions.

Let's imagine that you sell an employee health insurance program to a company. Your main contact at the client company is the vice-president of human resources, and you don't have access to other senior executives. When the time comes to renew the insurance policies, the CFO starts complaining about your prices, the CEO wants her brother in law to get a crack at the business, and the vice-president of sales is complaining about the dental benefits. Even if the final decision is left up to the vice-president of HR, these other decision influencers must be considered as your customers, because their impressions of you (or lack thereof) can affect your success. Recognizing these people as customers will ensure that, at later phases in this process, you will identify ways to create a positive experience of Brand Harmony for them. Even if you never gain direct access to them, you will be encouraged to think of effective ways for the vice-president of HR to translate your brand message to her colleagues.

Once you identify who the customers are who can help you reach your goals, you can focus on the actions that you need these customers to take. Be specific. Do you need 15 new customers to place initial orders of at least $5000 in order to reach your objectives? Do you need each of your existing customers to refer three new customers over the next 18 months? Do you need your largest customer to sign an exclusive sourcing agreement?

This is a very important phase, because it relates directly to the actual production of results. In the Brand Harmony Results Model it is customer action that drives success. Work through this phase by working backwards from the picture of success you have created, defining the detailed and specific customer actions that will create success for you. For example, if you had identified that you want to grow revenue from your top 100 customers by 15%, you can list out the different ways that can happen. Do you want them to purchase more of the same products they have already purchased? If so, will that happen by having them do more transactions, or more volume per transaction? Or, will you accomplish this goal buy persuading them to pay a higher price for those products? What about the purchase of other products in your line that they have never purchased from you? What if they were to make advance commitments to purchase in bulk volume?

Be willing to define some of the smaller steps you want customers to take that are prerequisites to a stronger relationship. For example, if you are looking to build a long-term, involved relationship with a prospective customer, it may seem daunting and unmanageable to focus on the actions you want them to take once they become a major customer. Instead, start by defining some of the initial steps you want them to take. For example, at this point in time you might only want them to agree to a meeting, or to include you in their next bid. Maybe you want them to award you a small, trial project that can demonstrate your talents to them. As with all projects that you undertake in your life, a clear focus on next actions is critical to your eventual success.

Pitfalls to Avoid in Phase 2 of Designing Brand Harmony

Here are some things to watch out for as you do the implementation steps related to Phase 2 of designing Brand Harmony.

- **Not letting go of pre-conceived notions.**

  Be willing to let go of preconceived notions about your customers that may prevent you from seeing them in a new light. We all create legends about our customers, and they're not always based on reality. Question everything you think you know.

- **Creating generic definitions of customers.**

  Avoid simplistic, superficial definitions of customers. As Lisa Fortini-Campbell recommends, gain an understanding of your customers in the way an actor gains an understanding of a character he is about to play. Don't confuse broad generalizations for the characteristics of individual customers.

- **Confusing proxies such as demographics and media habits with purchase characteristics of the customers they describe.**

  Be careful not to confuse proxies that make it easier for you to reach customers with the actual customers themselves. You may be able to reach a certain group of customers by advertising in a particular magazine, but that doesn't describe who they really are or why they would want to buy your product.

- **Defining customers based on the company's organization chart.**

  Your sales force may be organized geographically, but that doesn't mean your customers have to be. Additionally, your product managers may only pay attention to their particular products, but it may be important to define your customers by the way they use combinations of your products.

- **Failing to connect customers to actions and actions to business objectives.**

  The whole purpose of this phase of the process is to identify the customers and actions that will help you create your picture of success. Keep that picture of success at the top of your mind as you continue with the process of designing Brand Harmony.

Brand Harmony Implementation Step #5— Who They Are and What We Want Them to Do

Objective of this implementation step: Identify the customers who can best help you reach your goals, and identify what it is you want those customers to do.
Time required: ½ to 1 day

If yours is like most organizations, the most meaningful improvements in your performance will come from getting your customers to do certain things. Whether it is becoming a customer, staying a customer, becoming a better customer, referring colleagues, etc., customer action can improve the performance of most products.

There are two stages of this implementation step: 'who' and 'what.' Who are the customers that can help you meet your objectives, and what is it you need them to do?

Who they are

Make a list of the different components of your picture of success, which you created in Implementation Step #4. For example, your picture of success may have had the following component objectives for the following year:

- Retain 98 of our top 100 customers
- Grow volume from the top 100 customers by 15%
- Find 20 new customers in the aerospace industry
- Sell $1 million of new product X in Canada

Write each of these objectives at the top of a piece of easel paper which you affix to the wall. Now, with your colleagues, list in columns down the left side of each paper the customers who could help you realize each objective. In many cases you will need to include not only the actual customer decision makers, but those who influence their decisions.

In many cases you'll list groups of prospective customers ("The top 50 mining firms in Saskatchewan"), but you may also list an individual customer if that one customer can play a special role in helping your reach your objectives.

Don't feel limited to any specific number of customer groups. You can always consolidate them later. The purpose now is to identify who will help you reach your objectives. If there are many customer groups that can help you realize your objectives, recognize that fact.

What you want them to do

Now, to the right of each customer listed, write down what you would like them to do.

These lists should include definite and specific actions that help you reach success. Be descriptive. Be complete. And be accurate; make sure that the customer action you define is specifically directed at your picture of success, and not at some generic objective. Also, be sure to define the small steps you want customers to take as your relationship with them grows. By doing this you will identify many of the hurdles that you must cross as you and this customer become more involved with each other.

At the end of this step you should have a list of customer groups, and, for each of those groups, you should have a list of actions that you need them to take. Look for similarities and difference between them, noting common actions you are looking for across the groups, and differences in what you want them to do.

This is the kind of implementation step that you should always be revisiting, reworking and reconsidering. Like it or not, customers are moving targets, and as new data become available you should be willing to factor that new information into your thinking, looking for reasons to update your conclusions from this implementation step.

PHASE 3 FOR DESIGNING BRAND HARMONY:
DISCOVERING THE "DESIRED BRAND PERCEPTION"

Once you have a good idea of what you need customers to do to help you achieve success, you can move on to the next phase: identifying what it is that you want customers to think about you.

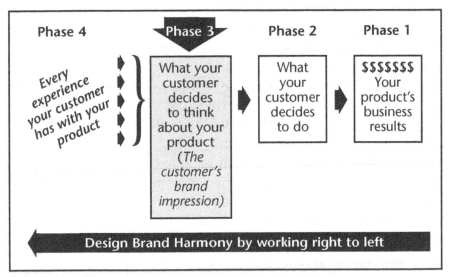

Figure 9. **The Brand Harmony Results Model**

If you magically appeared one day on earth as a fully functioning adult, one of the first things you would notice about your fellow humans is that there is a strong connection between what we think and what we do. This means that a customer's actions are driven by what that

> *"The ancestor of every action is a thought."*
>
> RALPH WALDO EMERSON

customer thinks. If we want to encourage customers to do things that help us achieve success, we must pay attention to what it is those customers think.

In Chapter 2 we said that "your brand is not what you say you are, but what your customer thinks you are." Think of your brand as the thoughts in your customer's mind that influence her behavior toward your product. What you say to her is not the direct cause of her behavior...it is what she thinks that causes her to act.

For this reason, I think we need to jettison the classical marketing concepts of 'brand positioning' and the 'USP' (unique selling proposition) in favor of a more customer-centered concept: the 'desired brand perception,' or DBP.

By thinking in terms of a desired brand perception, instead of the unique selling proposition, we are forcing ourselves to think from the perspective of the customer, not from our own perspective. What others think of us is a much more challenging barometer of who we are than what we think of ourselves. Look at it this way—isn't it much easier for companies to delude themselves than it is for them to delude their customers?

Our challenge at this point is to identify the desired brand perceptions that would encourage customers to behave in the ways we need them to behave. For the DBP to motivate a customer to act, it must pass three hurdles successfully:

- First, it must be something the customer *clearly understands*. He must say to himself, *"I get it!"*
  - *"I get it"* is a function of how strong the Brand Harmony is.
- Second, the message must be *meaningful*. He must not only say, *"I get it,"* he must say, *"I want it!"*
  - *"I want it"* is a testament to the message's relevance.
- Third, the message must *differentiate* the product. He must not only say, *"I get it, and I want it,"* he must say, *"I can't find it anywhere else."*
  - *"I can't find it anywhere else"* depends on how distinct the customer perceives the product to be.

A successful DBP must cross each of these hurdles. It must be able to be easily understood by your customers. It must be meaningful to them. And it must set you apart from competitive products in the customer's mind.

A good example of this principle is described by Josh Lesnick,

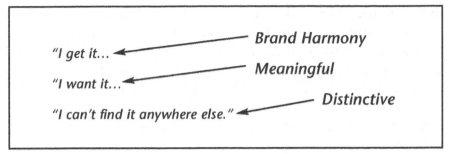

Figure 10. **Three Hurdles for a Successful DBP**

the architect of Starwood Hotels' highly successful Starwood Preferred Guest loyalty program: "We knew that people were very frustrated with airline and hotel loyalty programs because there are so many blackout dates that prevent them from using their miles or points for free stays or free flights. Also, these programs have so many rules and so much fine print it's hard to understand what awards you're entitled to. So, we decided to create a program that promised awards 'Anytime, Anywhere.' A simple program with no blackout dates would be easy to understand, and it would give people what they really want—free stays at any of our 700 hotels. And, it would truly set us apart from the competition." In other words, Lesnick wanted to create a brand impression of "Anytime, Anywhere," because it would encourage people to say, "I get it, I want it, and I can't get it anywhere else."

What happens if a brand impression doesn't make it over each of these hurdles?

"I get it"—We have already discussed what happens if customers don't "get" a brand message. Dissonant or disjointed product experiences are difficult for customers to understand.

"I want it"—If a brand's promise is not meaningful, customers will react to the only factor that always has meaning: price. Price is always a factor, in every transaction. The challenge is to create a brand impression that is so compelling it adds enough value in the customer's mind to enable you to command a higher price. If you're ever tempted to say, "All our customers care about is a low price," consider restating this as, "We haven't yet identified anything that is meaningful enough to our customers to command a

higher price." Even customers of BMW, Starbucks and Tiffany's care about price—they just care about enough other things that price is not the most important factor in their purchase decisions. Of course, you may determine that the best strategy for you is to be seen as the low cost provider...that's fine, as long as it is deliberate, and not a default strategy that happens because you have identified no other compelling reasons that customers should buy your product.

"I can't get it anywhere else"—If your marketing efforts don't lead customers to see your product as distinctive, any purchase interest that you create from those efforts may end up being shared with your competitors. A good example of this can be seen with online brokerage advertising. Each company's ads sell the general benefits of trading stocks on line, but don't do a good job of telling customers why their particular product is different from the competition. The result of this is that their advertising generates general demand for their product category, but not for the specific company promoted in the ads. You want customers to believe that the benefits they get from you can't be found anywhere else. Tom Peters is fond of quoting Jerry Garcia of the Grateful Dead when talking about the distinctiveness of a brand. Somebody once asked Jerry what the Dead were thinking back in the late '60's in San Francisco, as they were creating one of the greatest rock bands in history. Jerry said, "We didn't want to be the best at what we did, we wanted to be the only ones doing what we did."

Use these three hurdles as a litmus test for your desired brand impression as you create it. Aim high!

Additionally, as we discussed in Chapter 4, a customer can become more involved with a product if the thoughts he has about that product are rich and multi-faceted. We compared this to the way we react to great literary characters. Those characters whose personalities are complex and interesting are much more attractive and memorable to us than those that are flat and one-dimensional. We need to think of designing our DBP the way a writer thinks of crafting the personality of a great character.

Customers will inevitably perceive some sort of personality for your product, and a richer personality will do a better job of connecting with them and motivating them than will a superficial, simplistic personality. A customer can hang onto a rich brand perception, but a simple one will slip through his fingers.

To discover the best DBP for your product, you need to imagine what your customers *would* think about your product if you did an amazing job serving them and marketing to them. It's time to step into a dream world, to fantasize that you are reaching the success you pictured for your product earlier, and to envision what your customers would be thinking and saying in order for this success to become a reality.

> ## What *would* customers say if we did an amazing job?

To do this, you first need to get in the right mood. Shut off all of the self-critical thoughts going on in your mind such as, *"Our customers will never forget the problems they've had with us in the past,"* or *"Our senior management team will never allow us to do the things that will make customers love us."* Ignore the negative. Pretend! (You used to be good at it when you were a kid!)

Then return to the list of customer actions you identified in the phase 2 of designing Brand Harmony. For each group of customers, you identified the actions you would like them to take to help you achieve success. Now, for each of these customer groups, make a list of the laudatory, enthusiastic things they would be thinking and saying about you one year from now if you did a great job serving them. Write out full-sentence quotes. Imagine customer attitudes that don't yet exist. Imagine that they are passionate, raving fans of your product.

Let's look at an example which shows how the previous phases of the Brand Harmony Results Model can help you define you desired brand perceptions:

- Imagine that in your "panning for gold" implementation step (#3), you determined that there is an opportunity to receive much more business from your top 10 customers because you are selling only to a limited number of the potential purchasers in those companies, and each of them is buying only a portion of your product line.

- This led you to set an objective, when you defined your picture of success, that stated you would sell products from at least 5 different product lines to each of these customers over the next year, along with a related objective that you would grow business from each of these customers by a minimum 15%.

- You then determined that the key customer action you need for this to happen is that the plant foremen in these accounts endorse your product line to all departments in their plants, putting you on a preferred supplier list. Additionally, you decided that you need 80% of department supervisors who have never purchased your products to make at least one initial purchase.

- In order for this to happen, you determine that these plant foremen would need to think the following thoughts:
  - *"We're better off if we limit the number of suppliers we use and focus our business on XYZ Corp.'s products. That way, it will be easier for us to do maintenance, since their products all work in a similar fashion. XYZ can help us keep our plant maintenance costs down."*

- You determine that the departmental supervisors who have not used your product would need to think:
  - *"I should give XYZ a try. They seem to be really committed to us, and everybody else in the plant likes them a lot. And, maintenance should be easy since our guys are already so familiar with their products."*

In this hypothetical example, you connected the customer benefit of reduced maintenance costs to your goal of having customers buy more of your products. This was based on an understanding of your customers' needs and interests that you would have gleaned from your "panning for gold" analysis described earlier. Alternately, if that analysis had identified that your customers would focus on one supplier only if there were a cost advantage, you may have written these imagined customer quotes to say something like *"if we use all of XYZ's products we'll qualify for their discount program and significantly reduce our costs."* Or, if you had identified in the panning for gold analysis that there was a significant opportunity to capitalize on the competition's quality problems, you may want your customers to think, *"XYZ's products are much more reliable than the competitions'. We are better off if we expand our use of their products throughout the plant."* The earlier phases of the Brand Harmony Results Model can lead you to an appropriate DBP.

The selection of the best of these as the optimal DBP is not a matter of taste or aesthetics. It is a matter of identifying what customer thoughts will lead to the particular picture of success you have identified.

Once you determine what you would like customers to think, then you can pass it through the filter of reality and determine if this is a brand promise you can deliver. However, even at this stage you want to be careful about selling yourself short and abandoning a promising DBP because of your organization's shortcomings. If the DBP is strong enough, maybe it's worth shifting some priorities around to make it possible for you to deliver the promise inherent in that DBP. Remember, the DBP encourages customers to act in a way that drives your results. If a DBP is that compelling, be willing to change in order to live up to it.

Pitfalls to Avoid in Phase 3 of Designing Brand Harmony

Be sure to avoid these common problems as you craft your desired brand perceptions:

- **Failing to cross the three hurdles:** *"I get it, I want it, and I can't get it anywhere else."*

   Ensure that the DBP you define is ...

1. Easily understood by your customers

2. Meaningful to your customers

3. Seen by your customers as being different than what the competition offers

- **Falling back on price**

  Yes, your customers care about price. So do the customers of Starbucks and BMW. But, in both those cases, customers believe that they get enough other benefits to make price less of an issue. Be relentless in your search for benefits that are meaningful to your customers and different from what the competition offers. If customers believe that you deliver these benefits, they will care less about price.

- **Creating broad cartoon-like brand perceptions**

  The best brands are rich and multi-faceted; like the best literary characters, the personalities of great brands are multi-dimensional, interesting and complex. They have many facets that a person can hang on to, making it easier to classify and remember the brand impression. Create like Shakespeare, not like Hanna-Barbera.

- **Failing to describe your desired brand perception in your customers words**

  Take your voice out of the mix. As you discover your DBP, be sure to write out full-sentence quotes describing what your customers would say if you were doing a great job. Don't write what you would say, write what they would say. That way, you'll be forced to think from their perspectives, not yours.

- **Saying "no" too soon**

  This was also a pitfall to avoid in our earlier process of 'panning for gold'. When you speculate about what customers would say if you were doing a great job, there will be many times when you will be tempted to sell yourself short and say, "We'd never be able to do that." Ignore the temptation to self-criticize and edit these hypothetical customer raves. Saying "no" reflexively can stop you dead in your tracks. This is a phase of the process where you want to imagine a future that doesn't currently exist, so don't let the limitations of the present constrain you.

  Say yes. Don't worry, be happy.

Brand Harmony Implementation Step #6— What Will They Think of Us if We're Successful?

Objective of this implementation step: Discover the optimal desired brand perception (DBP) for your product.

Time required: ½ day to define the DBP's. Validation can take 2–4 days.

Most brand strategies focus on defining a 'brand positioning' or a 'USP' (Unique Selling Proposition). We've been discussing how the concept of the 'Desired Brand Perception,' or DBP, has more relevance for Brand Harmony than either of these two 'classical' branding terms. The reason for this is simple: Brand Harmony is much more concerned with what the customer thinks about your product than it is with what you say about your product.

In the previous implementation step you identified the customer action that will help you make your picture of success a reality. The question you now face is, "What thoughts in customers' minds will encourage them to take that action?"

To zero in on the optimal desired brand perceptions for your product, take these steps:

- Take one piece of easel paper for each customer group you defined in the previous implementation step. Write the name of that customer group and the actions you need them to take at the top of each piece of paper.
- Now imagine it is 12 months from now, and your branding efforts have been incredibly successful. As described previously, this is the time to be overly optimistic, and to shut out any negative, self-critical thoughts.
- On each piece of paper, write out complete sentence quotes that each of those customers *would* say if they were doing all of the things you want them to do. Fill up the

pages! Be complete and be descriptive. Use quotation marks, so that you will remember to create the quotes in words that your customers would use. (This differs from what you did in Implementation Step #3. That step focused on what customers actually think now. This step is about what customers *would* think in the future if things went well.)

- Reminder: Shut out the negative and be optimistic. You are writing quotes of what customers *would* say if everything were going perfectly well.

Make sure the quotes are aimed at the actions you need customers to take. For example, if the customer action you need is for them to switch from a competitor, make sure the quotes describe, in specific ways, why the customer thinks you are superior to that competitor. If you want customers to trade in their current models in exchange for upgraded, newer models, make sure that the quotes describe the advantages the customer sees in the new models.

Once you have a long list of quotes, it's time to zero in on your desired brand perceptions. As described earlier, a brand perception will more likely motivate a customer if it enables her to say, *"I get it, I want it, and I can't find it anywhere else."* Look at the list of quotes, and select those that best satisfy these three conditions.

Then, look for opportunities to consolidate the list, grouping quotes into common themes. Are there similarities among customer groups, or differences? Don't worry if you find that different customer groups need different DBP's. That will just indicate that you need to segment your communications to those groups.[8]

At the end of this implementation step, you should be able to write a description of what you want each customer group to think. Don't try to get it down to a simple 5-word slogan. Remember that richer thoughts lead to more involvement, and it's entirely appropriate for you to need a paragraph to summarize a customer's thoughts about your product. (We'll refine the DBP into a "brand essence" in Implementation Step #7.)

Ideally, it's best to validate your conclusions from this step with your employees, customers and, if applicable, distribution channel partners. Through one on one interviews or informal round table discussions with 4–8 participants, present the desired brand perceptions and encourage participants to comment. Pose the question by saying, *"Imagine if we were able to do a great job, is this what we would want our customers to think?"* and then read the desired brand perceptions.

In a one on one interview, let the respondent speak, probing as issues come up. In a round table discussion, don't have everyone speak right away. Instead, ask each person to write down their reactions and comments to the desired brand perception on a piece of paper. What you will find is that people are less influenced by the other respondents once they have committed their opinions to paper. Then, go around the room to hear what each person wrote, encouraging them to debate each other.

If you do one on one interviews, try to talk to at least (if applicable) 10 employees, 10 customers and 5 distribution channel partners. If you do round table discussions, try to do at least 6, split among the different participant groups. If the respondents don't agree with the DBP's you've created, or if they give you some new ideas, you may need to cycle through this implementation step one more time.

PHASE 4 FOR DESIGNING BRAND HARMONY: *ORCHESTRATING CUSTOMER EXPERIENCES*

Ah, but next comes the hard part. Now is the time to address the actions we take to create Brand Harmony in the minds of our customers, so that they will be more likely to create the brand perceptions we would like them to create.

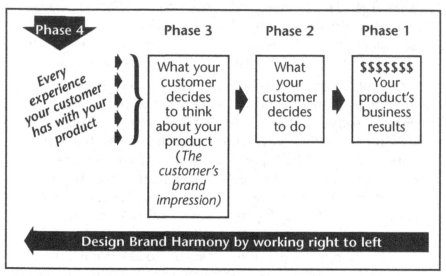

Figure 11. **The Brand Harmony Results Model**

A composer uses musical notes played by various instruments to create harmony. A chef uses different foods, herbs and spices. The raw ingredients used in the creation of Brand Harmony are the experiences customers have with products — which include not only the products themselves, but also any communications about those products. Like the chef or the composer, the marketer's challenge in creating Brand Harmony is to blend these ingredients into a composite mixture that has a special flavor or character. It is through the *orchestration* of a wide range of product experiences that customers can be encouraged to have the brand perceptions that we want them to have.

This requires a new mindset for marketers, since it requires a focus on the details of the everyday interactions between products and customers that marketing people have rarely paid much attention to. It requires you to see the beauty and importance of even the simplest and most mundane points of contact with your customers.

In 1886, Georges Seurat pioneered a new style of painting with his masterpiece, *A Sunday Afternoon on La Grande Jatte.* This style was called "pointillism," because of the way Seurat built a beautiful, complex image by combining many, tiny points of color. If you stand close to the painting, all you see are thousands of colorful dots and tiny brush strokes. But, as you move back, away from the painting, your eyes combine these dots into a complex, beautiful creation. Our challenge in creating Brand Harmony is much the same. All of the individual product experiences we orchestrate for our customers blend into an overall, beautiful picture, even though many are simple...nothing more than metaphorical dots of color. Simple things like the way a hotel doorman greets you, or the way an invoice looks, are not normally thought of as brand communications. But if we are inspired by Seurat's pointillism, we can see these interactions as important brand communications because of the way they blend with everything else the customer experiences to create a total picture.

Part of the art of creating Brand Harmony is to be able to foresee how these individual points of contact will blend into the overall character of the brand. I used to play music professionally, and an experience I had in a recording studio highlighted this for me. I was getting ready to record a guitar solo over some previously recorded tracks when the recording engineer, Mike Konopka, asked me to start playing my guitar unaccompanied. As I played, he started playing around with the sound of the guitar, turning various knobs and dials on my guitar and on pieces of signal processing equipment. After about a minute he had dialed in a sound I really didn't like very much. The producer on the session, Stuart Rosenberg, walked in the room, heard me playing and said "what a cool guitar sound!" I thought, "Ugh!" but said nothing. I had learned to trust the artistic judgment of Mike and Stuart without reservation, usually surrendering immediately to their choices. So I held my tongue as Mike started up the tape and I began to play with the rhythm guitar, bass and percussion tracks that had been previously recorded. As soon as I heard the guitar along with the other instruments, it sounded great. Now I understood why they wanted this sound. They were able to anticipate how it would blend with the other instruments, and weren't hearing my guitar in a vacuum. I wasn't able to picture how it would sound because I was focused solely on the sound of the lone guitar.

Harmony is relative. You can't judge the effectiveness of a product experience without considering how it will blend with the other components with which it is juxtaposed.

A marketing communication is never complete on its own. We can only understand its role when we understand how it blends with other communications. What a front-line employee says, what an ad claims, how the product actually performs; each of these on its own is incomplete and insubstantial. It is their relativity and contrast that matter.

All of these different product experiences reach customers in thousands of discrete pieces, like perfume that is atomized and drifts through the air, coming together to form a scent when it reaches a person's nose. However, the task of blending Brand Harmony has many challenges that the makers of scents don't need to consider. Unlike perfume, product experiences don't originate from one "atomizer." Some come from the marketing department, some from the customer service area, and some are created in the factory. To further complicate things, we can have great confidence that the ingredients of our Brand Harmony blend will *not* reach our customers in appropriate and consistent proportions, as they do with perfume, because there is much variability and serendipity in the way customers come into contact with products.

So, with all of this volatility in the way customers and products interact, how do we get these experiences to blend harmoniously? Is it coincidence? Is it luck? Is it the greatest feat of group improvisation imaginable?

Clearly not. Brand Harmony can't happen spontaneously any more than you could assemble a group of dancers and say, "Dance

Swan Lake, now!" The only way messages—tens, hundreds, or thousands of them—have any chance of blending harmoniously in a customer's mind is if those messages share a common source, something that directs their design and enables them to resonate with each other, something that allows them to be stitched together into a sensible whole in the customer's mind.

What is that 'something' that makes it possible for all of these varied experiences to be mutually reinforcing and blend into a clear brand impression? What is it that all of these different expressions of the product share?

Brand Essence—the "DNA" of your brand

I believe in something called "brand essence," the shared soul of the brand, the spark of which is present in every experience a customer has of a product. It is as if each expression of a product that the customer experiences could trace its genealogy to a common ancestor, the brand essence, which gives each of these expressions a character that can resonate harmoniously with all others. Brand essence is an underlying principle that guides all decisions and actions within the company that affect customer experiences. It is the common theme that helps the customer perceive Brand Harmony and piece these experiences together into the desired brand perception. It is the 'DNA' of all customer experiences.

> *Brand essence: The shared element that enables product experiences to resonate with each other.*

Think of the way DNA works in your body. Every cell in your body has the entire instruction set for your entire physical being within it. Yet each cell only expresses its own piece of the story. Eyelash cells "turn on" only the instructions for making eyelashes, and eyelid cells turn on only the instructions for making eyelids. As you grow into a whole person, these trillion cells work in harmony to create the complete you. The parts fit together beautifully—optic nerves connect to retinas, aortas connect to auricles, the hairline stops just above the ear. Your body 'makes sense,' and its cells all fit together beautifully, because each of these cells derives its essence from a common source, the DNA that they all share.

Now consider brand essence in your marketing. Similar to the way cells form in your body, every product interaction that the customer experiences should be designed, ideally, according to the guidelines of the brand essence. And we don't expect each product experience to tell the complete story of the brand. Unlike brute force branding, where we depend on ads and a relatively short list of other marketing communications to tell

> *We don't expect each product experience to tell the entire story of the brand.*

the entire story of the brand, Brand Harmony is built through many—hundreds, thousands—of mutually-reinforcing interactions that create an overall, meaningful story, reminiscent of Seurat's pointillism. It is the common brand essence, guiding the creation of every product experience, which enables these experiences to fit together so the customer perceives a sensible whole. Every interaction between a customer and a product plays a particular role in telling a piece of the story, perfectly complementing the others, but no single interaction is expected to communicate the entire message. For example, the employee at the front desk of a hotel may not use the same language or perform a task that is specifically described in the company's advertising; but, if the Brand Harmony is strong, the front desk clerk's actions will reinforce the message you saw in the ad. How could this happen? Only if a common source—the brand essence—served as the guiding principle in the creation of the ads and in the creation of the employee's service training.

Brand essence is the underlying "it-ness" of the brand, the source of all that the brand is, does and delivers. It is the glue that makes it possible for a customer to create an impression of the brand that is sensible. It is woven into every expression of a product that the customer experiences. Brand essence is not a tagline or a logo—those are nothing but expressions of the brand essence, as are ads, product features, and the smile of a front line employee. Brand essence is the genetic code from which an entire story can be woven, and the common element that helps a customer perceive Brand Harmony.

Brand essence is designed purely with the intent of encouraging customers to create desired brand perceptions. You should only begin to design it after you have defined your DBP. Brand essence is the elemental value of your brand that will—if all goes well—encourage customers to have the desired brand impressions we want them to have.

For one gourmet food shop, the essence of the brand may be that its proprietors' expertise will help you create memorable entertainment experiences. For another, it may be that the store provides you with the best selection of foods and cooking tools from around the world. For Starwood Hotels Preferred Guest program, as described earlier, the brand essence is that customers can use their points for free stays "Anytime, Anywhere." For a product I just saw on a TV infomercial, the brand essence is described by the product's claims to be the world's fastest fat burning supplement. If all customer/product interactions for these products are designed with the brand essence in mind, it is more likely that the Brand Harmony perceived by the customer will be powerful. In 1992, Bill Clinton's team created a very successful brand essence: "It's the economy, stupid." By using that as the campaign team's overriding value, they were able to create a series of mutually reinforcing messages that created a strong Brand Harmony in the minds of a large number of voters.

Brand Entropy

One of the most powerful forces in the universe is entropy, the tendency for systems to move progressively from states of organization to states of more disorganization and diffusion. You may organize all of the toys on a child's shelf, but over time they will inevitably end up scattered on the floor. You may get your colleagues started on the execution of a strategic plan, but, without constant attention, over time things fall apart and everyone starts to go their own way.

Without a strong brand essence to act as a glue, brand entropy will take over and the experiences your customers have with your product will become less consistent and more dissonant. The reason for this is simple—there are thousands of possible ways that any particular customer/product interaction can happen, but only a small number of those possibilities are appropriate for the Brand Harmony you are trying to create. Without a strong brand essence to hold things together, odds are that people in your organization will develop their own ways to interact with customers which, over time, will move further and further away from what their colleagues do. The natural tendency is to disintegrate, not integrate. When you create Brand Harmony, you are working against some powerful forces. A strong brand essence can go a long way to fighting these forces.

But, we still have to address a number of questions: Which customer/product interactions have the most influence on creating perceptions of Brand Harmony? What is the role of each, i.e., what part of the message should they each carry? What set of experiences will best connect with the customer?

Customer Touch-points—
Meet the Real "New Media"

For years, the brand-building media that advertising agency media departments have recommended to their clients have included television, radio, print and outdoor/place-based media. Along the way, practitioners of integrated marketing have broadened the "marketing mix" to include such options as direct marketing, public relations, promotion and sales. Now, it's time to take the next step by expanding the scope of marketing media to include the entire range of *touch-points* between a product and its customers. From the perspective of Brand Harmony, the customer service department takes its place right next to advertising in the ranks of marketing media. The recorded music customers listen to during interminable waits on the telephone for a representative "who is helping other customers" speaks louder than any radio commercial, no matter how clever that ad is.

Brand Harmony requires you to be prepared to have a marketing dialogue with a customer at any point you come in

> *Be prepared to have a marketing dialogue with a customer at any point you come into contact with her.*

contact with her. Brand Harmony requires you to take seriously the concept that "everything is marketing." In a world of Brand Harmony, marketing isn't a department; marketing is what the entire organization does.

Successfully creating Brand Harmony requires an organization to orchestrate all customer experiences so that the customer's overall impression is a sensible, motivating and meaningful whole. I call this process "Fully Integrated Marketing."

Why *Fully* Integrated Marketing?

"Integrated marketing" is a term that has been used to describe the coordination of various marketing communications tools, such as advertising, PR, promotion, direct marketing and sales. This kind of integrated marketing has been seen by marketing people as a tool to increase the effectiveness of their advertising—by adding a pinch of PR and a dash of direct mail, they could get a better bang for their marketing buck. In the traditional integrated marketing model, the integrating of various marketing communications tools is done at the discretion of the marketer. If you want to include direct marketing in your marketing plan, you can. If you don't want to, no one will force you to.

Brand Harmony, on the other hand, recognizes that it is the customer who does the integrating, not the marketer.

Customers get to decide for themselves which product experiences to consider as they form brand impressions, regardless of whether the company's marketing department has classified these experiences as "marketing communications." So, we need to move beyond integrated marketing to Fully Integrated Marketing, in which we recognize the need to orchestrate all customer experiences into a meaningful, integral story. Why? Because a customer has the prerogative to consider whichever experiences she chooses as she forms her brand impression.

Fully Integrated Marketing— customers do the integrating, not marketers.

Fully integrated marketing is our tool to create Brand Harmony. It considers every interaction with a customer to be a marketing interaction. It forces us to reconsider the role of marketing:

Marketing isn't just about sending messages to customers.

> **Marketing is about orchestrating the experiences customers have with products.**

> > **Marketing is a process of orchestration, not a series of one-way communications.**

What is the nature of these customer experiences that we plan to orchestrate? As we have said, they can happen at any point of interaction, or touch-point, between you and your customer. Relative to the media of brute force branding, the media of Brand Harmony are more numerous, smaller in scale and more interdependent. Consider a brute force branding media plan based on television, print advertising and billboards.

Fully Integrated Marketing—our tool for creating Brand Harmony.

These media are large in scale, are usually not dependent on each other to carry an overall message, and they usually say something to customers without giving customers much of a chance to say anything in return.

In contrast, the media of Brand Harmony, customer touch-points, are *granular, cumulative and interactive.*

Brute Force Branding	Brand Harmony
Big	Granular
Independent	Cumulative
One-way	Interactive

Figure 12. **The Nature of Marketing Media**

- **Granular**...The media of Brand Harmony can be as small-scale as a comment from a hotel front desk clerk or a typo in a VCR user's manual. They can include, but are in no way limited to, big, large-scale communications such as ads, brochures and banners dragged behind airplanes. They are numerous.
- **Cumulative**...They are an additive running tally, forming a cumulative set that the customer blends, if she chooses, into a composite brand impression.
- **Interactive**...Fully Integrated Marketing gives customers plenty of chances to speak back, since the media of Brand Harmony include many one-on-one encounters between the customer and representatives of the product. As we will address later in this chapter and in our "Be the Brand" discussions in Chapter 6, one-on-one interactions between customers and people representing the product

> *Traditional marketing communications are important...but not inherently more important than other customer touch-points.*

provide not only an opportunity but an obligation for inter-activity. We don't expect print ads to respond to us when we talk to them, but we expect a lot of dialogue from sales clerks.

How do traditional marketing communications, such as advertising, promotion, direct marketing and public relations, fit into this mix? They are an important, integral part of the mix, but only in the way they blend with the experiences customers have at other touch-points. Brand Harmony does not see traditional marketing communications as having a special, privileged role that is anything like the role they play in brute force branding. They are nothing but components of a cumulative brand impression, sharing the stage with many other of the "less glamorous" communications that occur during the day-to-day interactions between customers and products.

Our next step is to identify all of the relevant customer touch-points that will most influence customer brand perceptions. The trick to doing this is to have an "out of body experience" and imagine what it is like to interact with you, from the customer's perspective. If you were your product's customer, where, how and when would you encounter your product? Can you see things from the perspective of a customer as she encounters your product?

This is easier said than done! Brute force branding media plans are done according to the marketer's timeline, placing the right number of ad insertions throughout the budget year. We now need to abandon our marketing calendars and create a timeline according to the customer's sequence of interactions with the product. We need to think in terms of the *life cycle* of a customer's relationship with your product.

Life Cycle Marketing

Like relationships between people, relationships between customers and products develop over time. Communications that happen between old friends would not make sense in the early stages of a relationship, yet other communications are most appropriate during these early phases. The best way to identify the most important customer touch-points and, subsequently, to determine what part of the product's message is best communicated at each of those touch-points, is to map out the chronological steps in the life cycle of a customer's relationship with your product.

The most important factor to remember as you do this is that you are mapping out the life cycle of the customer's relationship with your product, not the life cycle of your product's relationship with the customer. The customer's perspective is what counts. Define activities and points in the life cycle by what the customer does at each point, e.g., "shop for the product," "make installment payments," "do maintenance on the product."

What you will find when you do this is very similar to what you found in our earlier panning for gold implementation step. As you map out the touch-points throughout the customer life cycle, the most important of these will reveal themselves. "Importance" can be defined in two ways:

1. How significantly experiences at this touch-point can influence customer opinions.
   - Examples:
     - Car rental companies know that the amount of time spent in line at the airport rental counter has a significant influence on satisfaction.
     - The wine list of a gourmet restaurant tells patrons a lot about the style of the restaurant.
2. How much room for improvement exists in your current delivery at this touch-point.
   - Examples:
     - You run a bookstore, and the people working at your information desk aren't knowledgeable about literature.
     - It's difficult to calculate shipping prices on your website.

As you map the series of touch-points that occur as your customers' relationships develop with your product, you will notice that a customer's experiences with a product can be classified into four chronological categories that occur throughout the life cycle:

- When the customer learns about the product
- When the customer goes through the process of buying the product
- When the customer uses or maintains the product

- When the customer tells others about the product, or just thinks about it

The touch-points that happen in these life cycle phases are the "marketing media" of Brand Harmony. The customer's brand impression is a cumulative running tally that she updates as new experiences occur throughout her relationship with the product. Let's explore each of these touch-point categories, with an eye to making a complete map of how touch-points occur as the customer's relationship with your product develops over time.

Touch-points During the Customer Life Cycle:
Learning About the Product

Among the ways customers learn about a product are advertising and all of the other traditional marketing communications, in addition to all of the other ways a company can inform prospective customers about their product: salespeople, signs on buildings, customer service reps, a snotty receptionist, to name but a few. But customers can also learn about a product from sources that don't originate within the company itself. These third-party communications can include press stories, word of mouth passed on by other customers, malicious lies told by competitors, etc. These must be considered, because the customer hears them in the overall tapestry of information about your product. If it can affect a customer's brand impression, Brand Harmony considers it to be a legitimate marketing medium.

An immediate reaction many people have at this point in the discussion is to say, "Hey, we can't control what other people say about us!" My reaction to this is, "Tough luck, your customers consider these part of the marketing mix, so you need to." Being aware of how third parties affect your Brand Harmony enables you to make other decisions that compensate for these effects as you blend the overall experience of Brand Harmony for your customers. Moreover, you may see opportunities to influence what these third parties say. For example, the techniques of Brand Harmony can be applied directly to your marketing to members of the press.

Touch-points During the Customer Life Cycle:
Buying the Product

The experience of buying a product offers a customer many opportunities to form opinions about that product. However, these customer touch-points are often not considered by those charged with responsibility for branding. Since consideration of the 'ergonomics' of the purchase process is usually neglected in the design of branding programs, significant dissonance can be created when customers try to buy a product. Long checkout lines, long telephone waits, labyrinthine call prompting systems ("press 7 for..."), incomplete catalogue product descriptions, unhelpful sales clerks, onerous credit policies—all of these color the customer's brand impression.

This neglect of the buying process as an important branding medium can be very damaging to a product's performance. Customers today not only have a choice of more products to purchase, they are offered many new ways to purchase those products. You can buy groceries at a corner store, a supermarket, off the internet, from a food co-op, or at Wal-Mart. You can buy a vacation from your travel agent, a tour operator, direct from an airline or hotel company or through your credit card; you can pay with cash or airline miles; you can buy over the phone, in person or on the Internet. As products have become more commoditized and purchase options have become more varied, customers have started to focus more attention on "how I buy," instead of basing purchase decisions exclusively on "what I buy." On the positive side, the result of this is that otherwise unremarkable products can be differentiated largely by the way they can be bought. On the negative side, many products suffer from cumbersome, obstacle-ridden purchase channels that add a damaging dissonance to the customer's impression of the product.

Understanding the interactions customers have with your product while trying to purchase it, and using this understanding as a powerful opportunity to reinforce Brand Harmony in the minds of your customers, is a critical component of success for any product.

Touch-points During the Customer Life Cycle: *Using a Product*

It is hardly a novel idea that customers form impressions of products when they use them. What we need to consider now, however, is that the act of using a product has gotten much more complicated, and that this impacts the way product use influences brand impressions.

Think of your computer. Using this product involves much more that typing on it. Setting it up, getting it working, calling tech support, installing a printer that isn't compatible, upgrading it, rebooting it after it freezes...all of these are palpable customer experiences that contribute to brand impressions. When you map out all of the ways your customers interact with your product through the processes of using it, getting it ready for use, maintaining it, fixing it, improving it, etc., you can find many points where Brand Harmony can be improved or degraded.

Brand Harmony forces us to recognize these many points of interaction between the customer and the product as branding experiences. Customers are continually updating their views of products they use and own, influencing not only their future purchases and involvement with the product, but their comments to other potential users of the product.

Touch-points During the Customer Life Cycle: *Talking or Thinking About a Product*

For a moment, consider something about which you feel passionate. You may really like it or you may dislike it. Maybe it's a movie, a TV show, a person you know or something going on in politics. Now, what would happen if you discussed your feelings on this topic with a friend or thought deeply about it for 5 minutes? Would your opinion evolve? Would you think differently about it after even such a short time?

Of course you would! Thinking and talking are very productive processes for people, enabling us to gain insights and enrich our opinions with very little effort. An author friend told me about a talk she gave, in which covered material from a book she had spent a year writing and had spoken on many times. She knew this material backwards and forwards, but as she spoke new insights and ideas came to her, which she shared with the audience. "I couldn't believe what was coming out of my mouth!" she told me.

Years of observing focus groups and conducting customer interviews have shown me that this happens with brand impressions of products. I sense, as I listen to people discuss the positive or negative aspects of a product, that they are saying things they have never thought about before. By talking about the product, they are refining and evolving their brand impressions.

This illustrates a collateral benefit from customer referrals. Every business wants its customers to refer friends and colleagues, because the referral of an existing customer has much credibility with a prospective customer. As an added bonus, however, the referring customer's own brand impression will be reinforced as he gives his friend an enthusiastic recommendation about the product. He not only persuades his friend, he persuades himself.

Brand impressions are anything but static. A customer's brand impression is a cumulative, running tally that is continually updated each time the customer has an interaction with the product or thinks about it. A thorough understanding of the complete set of touch-points your customers have with your product—including the most ephemeral thoughts that pass through their minds—will put you in a much better position to manage the experience of Brand Harmony you want your customer to perceive.

After mapping your customer touch-points, your next challenge is to organize these touch-points into a fully integrated tactical marketing plan. The purpose of this plan is to help you orchestrate the experiences your customers have in a way that best expresses your brand essence and creates Brand Harmony in their minds. As with traditional tactical marketing plans, you need to determine what media to use, and what message to communicate in each of those media. Choosing media in this case amounts to prioritizing your customer touch-points according to the criteria presented above—which touch-points most influence customer opinions, and those for which your delivery has the most room for improvement.

One thing you will notice right away, most likely, is that there are more touch-points screaming for your attention than you can possibly address. Don't be overwhelmed! You can't do everything at once, so don't drive yourself crazy trying to. Brand Harmony isn't like an on/off switch; instead, it is more like a dimmer switch. Do what you can now, and move on to the next level of priorities as you make progress.

Concurrently, you need to determine how your brand essence should be expressed at each touch-point. Remember our DNA metaphor: we don't expect every customer interaction to tell the entire brand story any more than we expect an eyelash cell to express every physical characteristic of your body. Identify the role you want experiences at each touch-point to play as they contribute to the overall tapestry of Brand Harmony. Your guiding principles are Brand Harmony and the desired brand perception—use these ideas to help you figure out the best way to orchestrate all product experiences in a way that will resonate with the customer.

This step of determining the proper message at each touch-point can also be overwhelming. If your situation is like most, you've recognized that you are creating a lot of dissonance in your customers' minds and have many problems to address in order to improve their experience of Brand Harmony. Don't panic! Recognize the entire set of issues that confront you, but then set a reasonable and prioritized plan for implementation.

Do You Hear What I Hear: Redux

The experiences any one customer has with a product are unique to that customer. No other person on the planet interacts with a particular product in the way she does; she has her own personal set of touch-points with the product, and she encounters them in an order and in contexts that are not duplicated by anyone else. She interprets this unique set of experiences by filtering it through her own personal set of biases and life experiences. The result: each customer's brand impression is her own. She creates a multi-faceted, rich picture of the brand in her mind that is as matchless as a snowflake.

What does this say to us as we plan to create Brand Harmony in the minds of these distinct, individual customers?

As discussed earlier, brute force branding allows us to get away with broad generalizations about customers, because advertising-based thinking about customers looks for ways to group customers into broad categories that correspond to the audiences of particular media. These generalizations inevitably force compromises, requiring us to assume that customers who share like demographic characteristics or similar media habits would also want to buy the same product. Generalizing broadly about customers is reasonable in a brute force, advertising-driven world, however, because advertising media don't allow much fine tuning. Advertising in mass media reaches many people with the same message, so we have to accept these compromises as an inherent part of using these media.

Creating Brand Harmony, however, both enables and requires a highly detailed look at individual customers' characteristics. At the heart of Brand Harmony is the notion that each contact between the product and a customer is part of a cumulative marketing dialogue that is unique to the product and that one customer. Many of those contacts are encounters in which the product meets the customer one-on-one.

These one-on-one encounters present both an opportunity and an obligation to personalize the delivery of the product or service to the needs of the individual customer. It is an opportunity because we can increase the relevance of the message to a customer if we talk to her personally, in a way that reflects her relationship with the product. It is an obligation because discerning customers will easily notice if we don't take this opportunity. When we are scrutinized by our customers across on ongoing series of encounters, many of them happening in real-time between employees and customers, we can't get away with the broad, generalized views of customers that work in an advertising-driven world. We're too exposed. Customers can see through any superficial, generic ideas we may have of them.

The last time I went car shopping I was surprised that no salesperson I dealt with wanted to accompany me on test drives. In each case they photocopied my driver's license, handed me the keys and told me to enjoy the ride. What a missed opportunity! Seeing their brands as iconic and immutable, they figured they'd just let the car speak for itself. Had they been with me on the test drive, however, they could have fine-tuned my experience in a way that would have led me to create a personal and motivating brand impression. By observing my reactions to the car as I drove, asking me what I liked and didn't like and querying me about my driving needs, the astute salesperson could have emphasized things I cared about and, potentially, neutralized some of my less positive feelings. As with our earlier example of Ruth deciding to buy a VW, I was forming very complex and multi-faceted thoughts about these cars as I shopped. By remaining back in the showroom sipping coffee, these salespeople neglected a chance to use one of the most important touch-points in the car buying process to their advantage.

As we've discussed, these personal, one-on-one encounters are part of an overall one-on-one relationship between the customer and the product, creating a personal brand impression for each customer. We will be better able to create a meaningful experience of Brand Harmony for a customer if our interactions with that customer reflect that unique view of the brand.

Recognizing that each customer can, potentially, have her own brand impression is a daunting realization. But consider the advantages for the organization that is not intimidated by this and can interact with individual customers in a personalized way that reflects the customer's unique relationship with the organization's products. The mind of each customer who comes in contact with your product contains a unique set of memories, feelings, disappointments and satisfactions about your product. And she brings to the encounter her own set of hot buttons, cold buttons, interests, desires and biases. The organization that can interact with this customer in a way that reflects these personal qualities will have a much better chance of connecting with her in a way that truly motivates her.

This is only possible if your 'customer sensors' are tuned in to discern an individual customer's personal brand impression. Listening to customers, sensing their feelings, discerning their motivations and interests...all of these are important if you are to adequately harness the power of Brand Harmony. Having the courage and equipment to do this is a key feature of success.

An organization successfully creating Brand Harmony in the minds of its customers is a society of listeners with an uncanny ability to respond in real-time to the things they learn about individual customers. Like many other changes needed to create Brand Harmony, this will be challenging for many organizations. It requires an unwavering commitment to a kind of customer focus they have never had before, well beyond the token efforts of customer attention for which so many companies congratulate themselves.

> *Assuming generic customer relationships in a world of Brand Harmony is like trying to paint a filigree pattern with a paint roller.*

The first step in this process is to jettison the beliefs and perspectives of customer homogeneity inherent in brute force branding, because assuming generic customer relationships in a world of Brand Harmony is like trying to paint a filigree pattern with a paint roller.

You must be willing to see every customer as unique, and you must create the "culture of customer curiosity" we discussed earlier. That culture is not only a mindset; it must be enthusiastically supported in every nook and cranny of the organization through processes, systems and explicit encouragement.

You must also look at marketing communications as an interactive process. Marketing communication isn't about sending messages to customers, it's about having a dialogue with customers in which you learn about the customer and increase the relevance of the brand message with each successive iteration of the dialogue. Active listening and observing are as critical to delivering a personalized brand impression as breathing is to speaking.

Each employee of the organization must recognize that his or her role is not just to serve a customer a cup of coffee, or fly her to

Salt Lake City, or sell her a new dress. The role employees play—a subject explored in the next chapter—is to interact with each customer in a way that contributes positively to that customer's view of the brand. To do this, employees must be capable of having 'out of body' experiences when dealing with customers, where the employee learns to understand what it is like to interact with the company and its products from the customer's perspective, and can react in real time to that perspective.

Most companies don't train their employees to see things from the customer's perspective. Look at simple things, like the way store clerks hand you change from your purchase by stacking the receipt on top of paper money, and coins on top of that. This is the most inconvenient way to receive money if you are a customer (especially if you're holding an ice cream cone), but it's the most convenient way for the cashier. Has anyone taught this cash register clerk to understand his job from the customer's perspective? If we don't train people to do simple things like give change in a way that is comfortable for the customer, how can we expect them to discern (and consciously contribute to) the customer's brand view?

Customers notice these kinds of things. In a world where each customer sees herself as special and unique, generic treatment rings hollow. Each customer has to believe that the product recognizes her uniqueness. If not, relevance will be diluted.

Personalization: The Universal Strategy

Personalization isn't just a nice thing that a few companies like Ritz-Carlton do. Where quality was once a universal strategy, personalization is *the* universal strategy in a world of empowered customers who use Brand Harmony to evaluate products.

Personalization has been a popular topic over the last few years, but most discussions of personalization quickly turn into conversations about technology, and how personalization can be automated now through powerful database and collaborative filtering tools.

But personalization isn't about technology. It's about recognizing that each customer has a unique brand impression, and our ability to persuade each of those customers is in direct proportion to our ability to recognize and react to those personal brand impressions as they are formed.

Tabasco Sauce To the Rescue

I remember once discussing personalization with a group of resort hotel general managers. They readily agreed that personalized treatment would be meaningful to their customers, but the task seemed too intimidating. "How can I possibly personalize for all of my customers, all of the time?" asked the manager of a large island resort. "I have 600 rooms, and the place turns over with new guests every 5 days, on average. How could we possibly keep up with it?"

"Simple," I replied. "You don't have to personalize for all of your customers, all of the time. Personalization is like Tabasco Sauce. A few well-placed drops can give an otherwise bland dish a robust flavor."

Like hot sauce, a little personalization goes a long way. We need to think of personalization as a prime ingredient in our Brand Harmony blend. Brand perceptions are cumulative running tallies, and small doses of personalization can have a powerful effect on the overall flavor of the Brand Harmony. Consider the resort hotel example. Let's say you check in at a resort for your honeymoon and five minutes later receive a call from the concierge:

"When you booked your vacation with us, you mentioned it would be your honeymoon. Let me know if you'd like me to arrange a secluded table in the restaurant, or if I can arrange a picnic on a nice beach away from the hotel for you. Also, when you booked your vacation, you mentioned you wanted to go horseback riding. Let me know if I can make that happen for you."

Most of the services the hotel will provide you during your stay will not be personalized. The towels and linens in your room will be the same as everyone else's. The food you'll be served in the restaurant will be off the same menu everyone else orders from. But a couple of small, powerful drops of personalization will give you the impression that this hotel understands you and your particular needs. When it comes to personalization, a little goes a long way, just like with Tabasco sauce.

But the Sauce Burns if It Spills

Of course, promises of personalization aren't enough. Brand Harmony requires a symphonic delivery, where each experience the customer has resonates with all others, despite the fact that these experiences originate within different points in the organization. If the hotel's restaurant blows it and places you next to a table of screaming kids, or the equestrian center never responds to the concierge's request to call you, then dissonance will sound loudly.

One of the prime tools of personalization that has evolved in the last decade is Customer Relationship Management or "CRM." Like the overall practice of personalization, CRM has degenerated into a technological discipline, with much of the focus on software and too little focus on how employees interact with customers. CRM should be seen as a set of tools to help create Brand Harmony, enabling the creation of a mutually reinforcing set of customer experiences that can be used to enhance the cumulative brand impression and drive business results.

If you talk to 100 people who have been involved in the implementation of CRM, it's likely that 99 of them will tell you that the software did most of what they needed it to do, but that their organization couldn't figure out how to use it properly. You'll hear how this department wouldn't input information, and that department didn't pay attention to what came out of it, and the employees of another department kept forgetting to use it. CRM fails if it is a computer task foisted on employees. To succeed it has to be viewed by employees as a set of tools that help employees listen to customers and react to what they learn in an effort to fulfill a greater goal: Brand Harmony.

Through years of listening to customers talk about products, I have observed that the recognition of unique customer needs and the ability to personalize responses are the most common reasons for both complaint and praise. Customers never like being treated generically, and they always hate when they are not listened to, no matter what the product.

Pitfalls to Avoid in Phase 4 of Designing Brand Harmony

Three implementation steps follow that will help you create an orchestrated Brand Harmony marketing plan. Watch out for these common problems that can dilute the effectiveness of your plan:

- **Using your calendar instead of your customer's**

    As you map customer touch-points, think about the life cycle of your customer's relationship with the product, not the life cycle of your product's relationship with the customer. For example, don't map the points where you send quarterly mailings to customers. Instead, focus on how receiving that mailing fits into the rest of the customer's relationship with your product. Think of touch-points from the perspective of the customer, not from your perspective.

- **Failing to consider all of the touch-points**

    Don't be afraid to think small. I won't buy another computer from Gateway because I couldn't get them to send me two tiny screws they forgot to include with my computer, even though I called them many times. You may think that's petty, but I think it's pretty typical.

    Customers have the prerogative to decide that any touch-point, no mater how small, is of major importance.

- **Failing to determine which touch-points are most important**

    The most important touch-points to your customer may not be those that have always seemed to be the most important to you. Be willing to rethink your idea of marketing media, acknowledging which touch-points can have the most influence on customer opinions.

- **Failing to recognize which touch-points, in terms of your delivery, have the most room for improvement**

    Question everything that is happening across all customer touch-points. Assess where you can do better, and commit to improving the way you deliver your brand promise at those points.

- **Dismissing touch-points over which you have no control**

    You may not be able to control certain experiences that customers have with your products, but you can plan to compensate for them. Avoid the temptation to say, "Well, we can't do anything about that, so let's ignore it." Instead, determine what you can do to counteract any negative experiences, whether they are things said by competitors, the press, former customers, or ex-employees.

- **Failing to define which part of the message should be communicated in which touch-points**

    Brand Harmony is built from complementary, not identical, communications. Look at the various components of your rich, multi-faceted desired brand perception, and determine where each of its components can be communicated. Don't try to tell the whole story at each touch-point.

- **Failing to have the focus, courage or equipment to personalize**

    Personalization is harder than treating all customers the same. However, each customer has a unique view of your brand. Embrace the challenge to see customers as unique... because they are.

Brand Harmony Implementation Step #7— Finding the Brand Essence

Objective of this implementation step: Zero in on the core values of your brand, defining the brand essence that will serve as the DNA of everything you do.

Time required: 2 hours (If you've done all of the previous steps, this should go quickly!)

You want to encourage customers to have the desired brand perceptions you identified earlier in Implementation Step #6, and you will do this by orchestrating all of the experiences customers have with your products. In order for the customer's cumulative perception of these different experiences to be harmonious, the experiences themselves need to share a common brand essence, which functions like DNA, carrying the core information, values and principles on which the brand is based.

Gather your colleagues together and write the desired brand perception(s) you have defined on paper affixed to the walls around you. What are the most compelling themes contained within them? What is the essence of these DBP's? Is it personalization? Is it price? Is it quality? Is it some combination of two or more qualities, as in "tastes great, less filling?"

We want the DBP to be rich and descriptive, but we want the brand essence to be tight and concise. Get it down to a short sentence, such as:

- The Kane County Cougars offer a professional baseball fan experience that is more fun than any other.
- Ritz Carlton is based on ladies and gentlemen serving ladies and gentlemen.
- Tom Peters Company invents the new world of work.
- Joe's Painting Service gets the job done on time.

These statements may look suspiciously like traditional brand positioning statements. They're not. They are values that help us create desired brand perceptions. They are the common ingredient that exists in every experience the customer has with the product, working as a glue to tie these experiences together in Brand Harmony.

Brand Harmony Implementation Step #8— Touch-point Mapping

Objective of this implementation step: To identify all the points of contact your customers have with your product throughout the life cycle of their relationships with your product.

Time required: ½ day to do an initial draft; more if your process is especially complicated or if you have many different customer groups. The process can generate many questions and issues you hadn't thought about, so figure as much as 2–3 more days to fully develop your touch-point map.

The marketing media of Brand Harmony include any and all points of contact between your customer and your product. This step will help you identify these touch-points so you can determine the best way to create Brand Harmony in the minds of your customers.

In Implementation Step #1 you did an initial audit of the Brand Harmony your customers perceive, and in the process of that step you listed many of these touch-points. In this implementation step you will complete that list and organize them chronologically according to the life cycle of the customer's relationship with your product, creating a "schematic" map of all touch-points. You should do this for each of the customer groups you have identified.

The most important issue to remember as we map these touch-points is to do it from the customer's perspective. Imagine all of the times an individual customer comes in contact with your product, not every time your product comes in contact with a customer. Think about what the customer sees, not what you see.

Touch-points fall into 4 categories:

- When the customer learns about the product
- When the customer goes through the process of buying the product

- When the customer uses or maintains the product
- When the customer tells others about the product, or just thinks about it

Put blank sheets of easel paper across an expanse of wall, overlapping them slightly so you can write across the seams. What you are going to do is draw, chronologically, the process that your customers go through as they interact with your product. (Preferably, choose a "war room" where you can leave the paper on the wall for a few days—or even weeks—as you develop your touch-point map.)

At the top left, write "Learning about the product," and underneath that list out all of the ways customers can learn about your product. Look at these as entry ways into a relationship with your product. Then draw lines going to the right, labeling what happens next. For example, if a customer learns about your product from an ad in the newspaper, what happens next? Does she call a toll free number? If so, draw a line from the ad to the words "call center," and then follow that customer's chronological set of experiences from there.

There will, of course, be lots of branches and criss-crossing lines; customers from each source feed into multiple next-steps, and each potential customer can take many different paths as they learn about your product. You may notice that these steps are convoluted and labyrinthine...what does that tell you about your prospective customers' experiences? For example, many companies I work with have been surprised to see, at this stage, how cumbersome it is for customers to learn about them from their telephone call centers or websites.

As you work your way through the steps that customers go through to learn about your product, move into the next phase, the buying process. Write "Buying the product" at the top of the sheet just to the right of where you have progressed mapping touch-points, and detail the steps that people go through to become your customers. Be sure to account for the many different ways people can buy your product.

After that, write "Using the product" on the top of the next adjacent empty sheet. Map out all of the interactions that happen after purchasing the product—including interactions with people in your organization– throughout the entire time the customer will own or use the product. In addition to actual product use, include repeat purchases, maintenance, upgrades, break downs, etc. If your product is a service, be sure to consider all of the times your customer enjoys the benefits of your service, not just the times you are actually performing the service. Since no two customers' experiences are the same, imagine multiple scenarios.

At the end of this process your paper should contain lots of arrows, lines and circles, and you should have many insights about the experiences people have as your customers. Likely, you will have newly-classified many customer interactions as branding experiences, even though you have never thought about them in that way before.

Brand Harmony Implementation Step #9—
The Orchestrated Marketing Plan

Objective of this implementation step: Identify the most important customer touch-points and define the message for each of them.

Time required: This can—and should—take a while! Spend a ½ day generating a rough plan, after which you'll be able to estimate the amount of work that lies ahead of you.

In the previous implementation step you created a map of the points of contact you have with customers. These touch-points form the marketing media of Brand Harmony.

You can also look at your inventory of touch-points the way a chef looks at the array of ingredients spread out before him as he prepares to cook. Or the way a composer ponders the sounds of the orchestra's instruments as he begins to compose. These are the ingredients of Brand Harmony, and your job is to orchestrate them in a way that helps your customers say, *"I get it, I want it, and I can't find it anywhere else."*

Most likely, your touch-point map contains more points of customer contact than you can possibly pay attention to at this point in time. This presents a challenge, since we've said that customers consider any and all interactions with your product when forming their brand impressions. The obvious course of action? Prioritize! Don't expect to eliminate all dissonance; instead, focus on improving Brand Harmony incrementally by identifying the touch-points that are most critical to your customers' brand perceptions.

Look at the touch-point map you created, considering two issues:

1. Which touch-points are inherently most important to your customers?

   • For example, a furniture company I worked with identified that delivery time was a "hot button" for nearly all customers.

2. Which touch-points are most in need of improvement?
   - Has your analysis uncovered some points of customer contact where you are seriously under-performing, such as customer service?

Brand impressions are built over time in a customer's mind, in much the same way that the plot of a novel unfolds in a reader's mind. How do you want your story to be revealed over time? Across the touch-point map on your "war room" wall, take notes about the things you want customers to understand at each point in the life cycle. For example, since it is impossible to tell the complete story of your brand at the early stages when customers learn about your product, what are the key components you want prospective customers to learn? What are the key things you want to communicate at the moment of truth when the customer first decides to buy your product?

Now, consider what you can do improve customer interactions at each of these touch-points, in order to express the particular part of the brand message you want to communicate at each point of contact. Remember our DNA metaphor ...no single customer interaction is expected to tell the entire story of the brand. Your goal is to orchestrate interactions to create a cumulative brand impression.

Also, remember what we have said about personalization. At which touch-points are you best able to learn about the personal characteristics and interests of individual customers, and provide an experience that will be appropriate for that customer?

What you are doing is creating a *fully integrated marketing plan* that considers every customer interaction to be a marketing interaction. This is a tall challenge, and don't expect to finish it in one day. Use this implementation step to get you started, but continue to work hard, to continually look for ways to improve your interactions with customers and improve their experience of Brand Harmony. Once you improve the customer experiences at high priority touchpoints, move on to others. Look at Brand Harmony as something that can always be improved, and look at your points of contact with customers as the places where you can make that improvement.

6

Be the Brand!

A number of years ago, I was getting ready to board the 5:00 PM American Airlines flight from Dallas to Chicago. It was a hot day in August, and everyone in the gate area looked weary from a day of meetings and the oppressive Texas summer weather. As I made my way through the boarding line, I noticed that the guy in front of me looked especially haggard. He was trying to juggle a garment bag, a large legal document case, a jacket and a piece of carry-on luggage. Because he didn't have a free hand, he was holding his boarding pass between his teeth.

When he came to the front of the line he dropped his bag and handed the boarding pass to the ticket agent. She looked at him in disgust and said very loudly, "Ugh! That's disgusting! How would you like it if I handed you something that was in my mouth?"

As the man tried to apologize, the gate agent said, "I hate it when people do that!" Her voice remained loud, and by this time she had captured the attention of everyone within earshot. "Yich!" she continued, as she inserted the boarding pass into the automatic ticket reader, dramatically holding it by the corner with only the tips of her thumb and index finger. "It's sickening. What do people think, spitting all over their tickets and then handing them to us?" The man looked humiliated and beaten as he proceeded down the jetway. The gate agent then looked at me, smiled, and said, "How are you today?" as if nothing had happened.

A very clear picture came into my mind as she took my boarding pass and wished me a good flight. For years, American Airlines had spent a lot of money showing me television commercials that promised "Something Special In The Air." At that time I was a Platinum member of their frequent flyer club, so I frequently received special offers from them in the mail and warm chocolate chip cookies on the plane. But, despite all of their efforts to win my loyalty and persuade me how wonderful they were, the actions of this gate agent spoke louder to me than anything else I heard from them. As far as I was concerned, she was the American Airlines brand.

For better or worse, people are the most effective communicators of brand messages. This is because customers are more attuned to interactions they have with other people than they are to interactions with inanimate objects, such as full page ads, brochures and web pages.

If you look at the entire set of customer touch-points for your product, you'll see that virtually all of them are strongly influenced by people who work in your organization, either directly (e.g., a front line employee with customer contact) or indirectly (e.g., a person in your shipping department who packs the product into a box). In order to create Brand Harmony, it is critical for people throughout your organization to *Be the Brand,* which means that they need to understand their personal role in creating Brand Harmony, and they need to act in a way that supports that role.

What does it mean to *Be the Brand?*

Don't Confuse "Be the Brand" with "Service with a Smile"

A president of a professional services firm once said to me, "Steve, what's so new about this Be the Brand stuff? We've been telling our receptionist to be nice for years." My reply was that if the firm's brand promise is "We'll be nice to you" then the receptionist is right on strategy. Most likely, however, the firm's brand promise aims higher than that. "Be the Brand" is about much more than generic "good service." It is about employees displaying a particular kind of behavior that supports the brand strategy. If the firm's brand promise revolved around expertise in their field, the receptionist could be trained to ask a few qualifying questions so that the call could be routed quickly to the right expert. If the brand promised personal service from an account manager who knows you intimately as a client, the receptionist could be provided with a list of all client/account manager relationships, and could be trained to connect the client with their personal representative as seamlessly as possible, even if the account manager is lining up a putt at his local golf club.

> *"Be the Brand" isn't about good service, it's about a particular kind of service that supports the brand strategy.*

All Employees Need to Be the Brand

Every employee in a company, ultimately, has an effect on the customer experience. Of course, front-line employees who meet customers face to face or on the phone have the most direct impact. But I am convinced, after years of working on Be the Brand programs, that all employees, even those who never meet a customer, can have a positive impact if they learn to Be the Brand. A few months ago I developed a new brand strategy for a manufacturing firm, and our Be the Brand program included workers in the plant whose job was to pour hot liquid urethane into molds. These employees were many steps removed from the end customer, and in most cases did-

> *Even employees who never meet customers can Be the Brand.*

n't even have a good idea of who the firm's customers were. However, they were very articulate in describing how the brand strategy was affected by the jobs they were doing. In fact, based on input from these workers, the company's entire inventory process was changed in order to help the company fulfill its brand promise.

Do Employees Want to Be the Brand?

My experience has shown that employees, at all levels, are usually eager to Be the Brand. It is exciting for them to see how their jobs fit into a big picture that includes advertising and other communication efforts. In most companies employees feel disassociated from their organization's external advertising, because no one has shared the advertising strategy with them and helped them see how their jobs relate to it. But I have often seen them get very excited when they see how their jobs fit into the organization's overall marketing strategy.

As part of a brand strategy project for Wyndham Resorts in 1998, I worked with Wyndham's marketing, human resources and operations people on a Be the Brand training program for the company's resorts in the U.S. and Caribbean. In the Be the Brand training session in Jamaica, employees spontaneously started singing their country's national anthem, and at the start of the second day of training at the Wyndham Resort in Aruba a bunch of employees asked to perform a song they had just written. To the tune of "We Are the World," they sang "We Are the Brand." What these employees were saying was, in essence, "finally, somebody recognizes that what we do is important, and they're helping us figure out how make the best contribution possible."

Another company for whom I worked on an extensive Be the Brand program is Equity Office Properties, a company that owns and leases 124 million square feet of office space. Equity Office's front line employees eagerly embraced the idea that they are the best marketing program the company has. In fact, the employees who were consistently the most eager to Be the Brand were the building maintenance engineers. One, James Brady, was nicknamed

"Brand Boy" by his fellow employees, due to the fervor with which he approached being the brand. Equity Office building engineers 'get it.' They are involved with customers all day, every day, and they were thrilled to be able to be part of the company's overall marketing strategy.

Photo credit: Levi Yastrow

James "Brand Boy" Brady

Interestingly, there seems to be an inverse relationship between rank and readiness when it comes to Be the Brand programs. Front line and "lower level" employees are usually very cooperative and eager to make these programs work. When Be the Brand programs don't work, the fault can usually be traced to senior management.

Success Factors for Be the Brand Programs

Here are three factors that can spell success—or in their absence, failure—for Be the Brand Programs

1. Make sure everyone *understands* how to Be the Brand

   A few years ago I was speaking with a United Airlines flight attendant. The airline had just launched a new mega-advertising campaign, "United Rising," a campaign which described United as an airline that was truly focused on providing a better level of service. I asked her what the airline had done to coordinate the campaign's launch with flight attendants and gate agents, who meet more than 1 million customers every week. "Nothing," she replied. "We saw it for the first time on TV, just like you."

   A few months ago, while I was shopping for necessities like shaving cream, batteries and toothpaste, a Walgreen's cashier handed me a receipt that had printed on it, "Hi, I'm Robert. I'm here to serve you with our Seven Service Basics." This interested me, for obvious professional reasons. I looked up from the receipt—yes, his name badge said "Robert"—and I asked him what the Seven Service Basics were. He looked back at me puzzled, and I showed him the receipt. He said, "Wow, I didn't even know that was there." "Do you know what the Seven Service Basics are?" I asked. "I have no idea," was his reply. Over the ensuing weeks I experimented on other trips to Walgreen's. Similarly, Barbara didn't know she was being quoted on the receipts she was handing to customers, nor did Rajiv or Carla. None of them knew the Seven Service Basics.

In both of these cases, companies had created corporate marketing programs that related directly to the experience customers have with their employees. In each case, the company forgot to tell its employees.

Brand Harmony can't be successful if employees don't understand how to Be the Brand. To accomplish this, you first have to share your overall brand strategy with employees throughout your organization. Then, work with different groups of employees to help them define what it means for them to Be the Brand as they do their particular jobs. Be sure to make this last step a cooperative, joint effort. By allowing employees to co-author the personal steps they need to take to Be the Brand, you will have a more effective program. For one, they know more about their individual jobs than you do, so they are in a better position to identify specific ways that they can Be the Brand. Moreover, participating in the process will increase their sense of ownership, and a sense of ownership is the surest way to increase their commitment. As Harvard's president Lawrence Summers once said, in the history of the world no one has ever washed a rental car. Make this a program everyone in your organization feels that they own.

2. Make sure everyone can Be the Brand

I once worked with a hotel company that had determined that employees had to be empowered to make on-the-spot decisions in order to fulfill the chain's brand promise. The president of the company related to me a conversation he had with a front desk clerk. The clerk had described an unpleasant encounter with a customer, where the customer claimed that he had been quoted a rate $25 below the rate that was shown on the computer at the hotel's front desk. The clerk's personal opinion was that it was in the best interest of the company to honor the lower rate, but the rules required her to get permission from her general manager to change a room rate more than $20. The general manager was nowhere to be found, so the clerk was unable to make the change. The hotel company president immediately changed the policy after hearing that story.

Be the Brand programs will fail if employees are told what to do, but are not able to do it. This can happen if policies and procedures get in the way of an employee's efforts to Be the Brand, as in the story related above, but it can also happen if the company's operational systems aren't sufficient to support employees' efforts to Be the Brand.

3. Stick with it!

By far, the most common reason Be the Brand programs fail is that companies don't stick with them. Just when employees are starting to 'get it,' the guys at the top get bored and want to move on to something else.

With brute force branding, you can have your spring ad campaign, followed by the summer campaign, followed by the fall campaign, and they don't necessarily have to have anything to do with each other. However, as you try to create Brand Harmony, you can't change your strategy every few months. The creation of Brand Harmony requires the involvement of everyone in your organization, and schizophrenic changes of strategy will confuse everyone.

Sure, the strategy can evolve, and you can have employees emphasize different aspects of the brand promise at different times through their efforts to Be the Brand. But each of these changes must be seen—by employees and customers—as a natural evolution and growth of that brand promise.

The Power of A Company's Myths

I once was on a Southwest Airlines flight where, during our taxi prior to takeoff, the flight attendant turned the safety announcements into a comedy routine. It was hilarious. Was this flight attendant doing this of his own accord, or was there something about Southwest Airlines' culture that encouraged him to do this?

In building Southwest Airlines, founder Herb Kelleher created a *myth* around the company that employees believed in. This flight attendant may have improvised the specific words of his announcement, but he was doing it within the context of Kelleher's myth of what Southwest Airlines was. The Southwest myth served as a common frame of reference for Southwest employees, enabling them to Be the Brand in a way that created an experience of Brand Harmony not found on other airlines.

For eons, communities have used myths as a way to forge a common understanding of the complex world around them. In his book, *Sacred Fragments*, Neil Gillman describes myth as an "attempt [by communities] to discern specific patterns in their experience, and to shape these patterns into a meaningful whole that gives order to the world". "Myth", he continues, "lends integrity and identity to a community, generates loyalty to its unique destiny, motivates behavior and establishes deep and lasting affective impulses."

In modern usage, we have come to think of myths as stories that aren't true, but this isn't the meaning of myth that Gillman is speaking of. Gillman isn't concerned with the veracity of myths, only their power in holding communities together. Myths, he writes, are the "structure through which a community organizes and makes sense of its experience." As Stephen Palmquist, a professor at Baptist University in Hong Kong writes, "the term 'myth' will refer to any belief whose meaning is so intimately connected with a person's way of life that the person never considers asking the question 'Is it true or false?'"[9]

A company's myths are the common beliefs that its employees have that guide their behavior. If the myth is well understood by employees, it can be a powerful influence on their behavior—for better or worse. If a company is failing, for example, a strong myth of doom and gloom can arise, causing employees to behave in negative ways. If, however, a community of employees share belief in a myth that makes them feel proud to be part of their team, it can translate into powerful, constructive actions, like I witnessed on Southwest Airlines.

As Gillman writes, "the issue is never myth or no myth, but which myth." Your employee culture will contain many myths, and your challenge is to nurture myths that encourage employees to Be the Brand in an appropriate way. Similar to everything we've said about how customers create brand impressions, employees will not automatically believe everything they hear from the company. Their myths will form from the fabric of their experiences working for the company, and your challenge is to create a total work environment that resonates with the values of your brand. If your brand promises a speedy response to customers, be sure that you react quickly to employees' questions. If delivery of your brand promise requires employees to be experts in a certain field, be sure to have reward and recognition systems in place that acknowledge the development of that expertise.

This won't happen automatically. The challenge is a fully-integrated internal marketing program, aimed at creating Brand Harmony in the minds of employees.

Internal Marketing—More Than Ever

In many companies, the person charged with internal communications is a junior person working in the Human Resources department, whose primary responsibility is making sure that all employees get the latest information on insurance benefits and the office Christmas party.

To have any chance of creating Brand Harmony, we have to aim much higher. We have to look at internal marketing as some of the most important and serious marketing we have to do.

And we need to recognize that internal marketing comes first, before your marketing to the outside world. If your employees don't understand and believe in your brand, there will be no chance that your customers will be able to understand it.

I once shocked a client by telling him that if he made me choose between having his marketing people communicate to customers or to employees, I would choose that they focus their efforts on employees. His company acquires new customers through a sales-driven process, and the company's customer relationships last for many years. This means that employees have a much larger effect on customer brand impressions than any brochures, ads or press releases created by the company's marketing department. If employees 'get it,' I told him, marketing to customers will follow naturally because employees will interact with customers in a way that reinforces the brand. Luckily, no company has to make this kind of drastic choice. But most companies could benefit by shifting a significant portion of their marketing focus to their own employees.

Tom Peters Company describes this as the need to "fuse an indelible connection between the employee and the brand." They describe the need to build the "Brand Inside" if you ever hope to have the "Brand Outside" make sense to customers.

Internal marketing is much more than training. It goes beyond the "how to" and aims to help employees understand the "why." It doesn't just concern itself with job tasks. It aims to build credible, shared belief in the myths that surround the brand.

> ### *Internal marketing —it's serious marketing.*

To make internal marketing work, we have to remember that it is *marketing*. Like customers, employees will integrate all contacts with your company into a composite brand impression. Just like customers, your employees have brand impressions of your company that affect their behavior. To encourage them to have the "right" brand impressions—ones that encourage them to Be the Brand in an appropriate way—you need to create Brand Harmony in your employees' minds, ensuring that all communications to them are mutually reinforcing. If employees perceive their own Brand Harmony, they will be more likely to believe in the brand myth and behave in a way that contributes to customers' perceptions of Brand Harmony. Just as with customers, every interaction your organization has with an employee has the potential to change that employee's brand impression. Everything employees hear from the company, whether it is an official employee communication or what employees witness through the company's actions, influences their ideas about the company and what they are supposed to do to Be the Brand. An internal marketing program that starts with a big kick-off party and isn't followed up by substantive and sustained action will fail.

To create your internal marketing program, work through the Brand Harmony Results Model by following the implementation steps included in chapter 5, only consider the employees of your organization to be the customers to whom you are marketing. What is an appropriate picture of success for your internal marketing? What do you need each group of employees to do? What thoughts—"internal brand impressions"—do you want your employees to have? What internal marketing activities, as part of a comprehensive, fully integrated plan, will encourage your employees to have those impressions?

And remember to involve everyone in the company in internal marketing programs. Don't just focus on the front-line and hourly staff. Managers and supervisors, senior management, the board of directors and the company's shareholders all need to understand and believe in your brand strategy so that their actions support it. Especially don't forget your company's management! When a front-line employee forgets to Be the Brand for five minutes, he may damage the brand impression of one customer. When the boss of many employees forgets to Be the Brand for five minutes, she may make decisions that can adversely affect the brand impressions of hundreds or thousands of customers.

Marketer as Orchestra Conductor

What is the role of marketing people in this process?

For many years, marketing people have focused their efforts on communicating with the world outside of their organization. Creativity, a strong intellect, good analytical skills and a large budget were the primary ingredients for success. With only a handful of colleagues, including a well-compensated ad agency, a marketing executive could implement campaigns that reached millions of customers. Like a small team of guerrilla warriors, this group could get their job done without much distraction from the rest of the organization.

Brand Harmony, with its reliance on the involvement of people throughout the entire organization in the marketing process, requires a different role for the marketing executive. Her role is no longer limited to communication with the outside world. She is no longer like a soloist in the spotlight, whose work is seen by millions. Instead, she is like an orchestra conductor, coaxing and encouraging a set of fine performances from a large group of talented artists. Where she used to be able to give immutable directives to her ad agency, she is now faced with the challenging task of persuading people throughout her organization to Be the Brand as they live out the company's marketing strategy in the course of doing their daily jobs. The marketer is only responsible for delivering a small share of external messages, but she plays a critical role in preparing others to deliver the majority share of those messages.

This new role represents a different kind of leadership than what many marketing people are used to. It requires them to persuade people within their company who are not under their direct control. A lofty title and the power to hire and fire may have been enough in the past to motivate employees and ad agencies; these powers will have little effect on motivating the employees who work in departments other than marketing. The marketer's success depends on her ability to persuade all people in her organization to do their jobs according to the framework of the brand strategy. Internal marketing becomes one of her most important responsibilities.

The internal customers that she must persuade exist at all levels and all points in the organization, from employees meeting customers on the front-lines to senior executives exercising command and control from corner offices. Marketers need to lead people who are up, down, and sideways from them on the organization chart. Their success depends on their ability to persuade people to Be the Brand.

Bigger Isn't Better

All happy families are alike; every unhappy family is unhappy in its own way.

So starts *Anna Karenina,* the great novel by Leo Tolstoy. Happy families are happy because all of the things required for compatibility and domestic harmony are in place. The parents agree on issues of child rearing, discipline, religion, sex, lifestyle, financial priorities and other issues, and the children cooperate as is required of them, adding to the family's bliss. But, if only one of the many factors required for family happiness is missing, an unhappy family will appear, with its own unique story and set of troubles.[10]

So too with branding...

Successful Brand Harmony requires an entire organization to work together in pursuit of shared goals. For this to happen, many things have to be right. If, however, any one of a million possible issues within the organization impedes this cooperation, the customer will perceive dissonance. Like Tolstoy's ideal happy family, it's hard to ignore disunity, no matter what form it takes.

Brand Harmony requires what Jesper Kunde calls "Corporate Religion." The entire organization has to buy into the strategies that create Brand Harmony, as if it were their unquestioned way of life. The brand strategy must serve as a frame of reference that guides all actions and decision-making. The strategy can't be used only when convenient and discarded when the next new idea comes along.

What kinds of organizations can do this?

In the heyday of brute force branding—the 1950's through the 1970's—size mattered. The mass manufacturing economy rewarded big companies with profits through economies of scale, and those companies used mass marketing to sell their products. Simply put, bigger was better.

This bias towards bigness sticks with us to this day. Most lists of the 'best' brands that we see in the press are nothing but a list of the biggest brands. Is big still better?

No.

In a world of Brand Harmony, the playing field has been leveled and smaller companies can now compete in a way that they never could before. After all, it's much harder to get 50,000 employees to Be the Brand than it is to get to 500 or 50 employees to Be the Brand. The advantage that large companies had in a mass manufacturing world that was driven by brute force branding is gone. It's much easier for a small company to orchestrate a customer's total set of experiences to create a sensible, meaningful and motivating Brand Harmony.

If you are a small organization, this is good news for you. You can now compete with your larger competitors in a way that you never could before. The branding principles described in this book favor you over big companies, and they are more relevant to the way you interact with your customers. You may not sell as much product as the big guys, but the good news is that you don't have to. You can use Brand Harmony to create and retain customers much more profitably than the big guys can.

If you are a large organization, things have gotten tougher. You can no longer count on sheer muscle and brute force to win the competitive game with companies smaller than you. You have to work hard to orient your entire organization toward the pursuit of creating Brand Harmony.

The ability to get your organization in sync—and keep it there—as you create an experience of Brand Harmony for your customers is the true competitive advantage that will enable companies, of whatever size, to best realize the picture of success they have for their products and organizations.

Affiliates, Franchisees, Dealers, Contractors, Referrals and Brothers-in-Law

Imagine you're a lawyer. Your accountant is playing golf with someone who describes a legal problem he's having. Your accountant knows that this area of law is your specialty. What do you want him to say to his golf partner about you?

Chances are, he'd probably just say something like, "I have a friend who does that kind of work." Wouldn't you like him to say something more compelling than that? What if he described you in a way that would make his friend say, "Wow. I gotta call that guy!"

There are many times when people who don't work directly for your organization are in a position to communicate your brand message. Just like with direct employees, they can have a powerful influence on customer's impressions.

In certain cases, these people are actually representing your product. For example, consider employees of dealers or franchisees. They may get their paycheck from a franchisee, but customers may see them as directly representing the franchisor's brand. Or, what if you run an office building with security guards provided by an outside firm? Won't customers assume that they represent you, and blend the experiences they have with the security guard into their overall brand impression of your company? For these cases, you need to extend your internal marketing program to include these people, in a way that will encourage them to Be the Brand in an appropriate way. It may be more difficult than with your own employees, and the message you give them may conflict with what their direct employer tells them, but it is critical that you meet this challenge.

If you make a product that is sold by third-party retail stores, you face a similar challenge. How can you encourage the stores' salespeople to recommend your product or service disproportionately to other products? Can you help them understand your brand in a way that helps them communicate to their customers why your product is the best option? Like other customers, these salespeople will form impressions of your brand according to the principles of Brand Harmony. Every interaction with your company will contribute to the salesperson's impression of your product, and will influence the actions she takes (or doesn't take) on your behalf. Consider these retail salespeople just as you would consider any customer group to whom you need to market. Apply the Brand Harmony results model, and create a fully-integrated marketing program that will create the appropriate Brand Harmony in their minds.

In the cases of third-party referrals, as in the story of your accountant on the golf course, or your brother-in-law, your challenge is to arm your referral sources with a clear way to communicate your brand essence. Many professional service firms depend on referrals for most of their business, but very few of them do a good job of helping those referral sources tell a good story. Consider third-party referral sources as an important customer group to whom you must market your brand, and create a fully-integrated marketing plan to create an appropriate Brand Harmony in their minds. Their enthusiasm and sincere interest in helping you are important, but aren't enough to make their referrals as effective as they can be. Use the same techniques we have described in Chapter 5, applying the Brand Harmony Results Model to your referral marketing:

- Define the success you want in terms of the kinds of business you hope to generate from referrals, and then define the specific action you want your referral sources to take.

- Next, determine the desired brand impression you want referrals to have. This should be related to your core DBP, but has to also reflect something meaningful to the referral source. What's in it for the person referring you? For example, if your accountant refers you business, he needs to be motivated by more than an understanding of your brand. Do you want his brand impression of your product to be that referring you will make him look better to his clients? Or should it be that he can earn referral fees from you? Clearly, these would suggest different approaches.

Then, determine how you will communicate to these referral sources. Think of orchestrating the experiences of referral sources as similar to how you've done this for your other customers. What is the life cycle of the referral sources' relationship with you? How can you help him learn more about you? How can you help him best communicate your message when the time comes to do so?

7

The Will to Create
Brand Harmony

You've designed a program of Brand Harmony for your products. Your people are ready to Be the Brand.

Now ask yourself: Will you do it? Do you have the will to create Brand Harmony?

First, let's make sure we understand what your choice really is. It's not between Brand Harmony and some other marketing technique. Brand Harmony isn't a discretionary marketing program you can opt to ignore; Brand Harmony is a description of the way your customers are evaluating you at this very moment. Your choice isn't between doing Brand Harmony or not doing Brand Harmony. Your choice is between having your customers perceive Brand Harmony or perceive some sort of brand dissonance.

If you choose to create Brand Harmony, you are choosing to make it easier for your customers to be involved with your products. But you are also choosing a challenging road. I recommend you take that road, but it is a road that requires commitment and will. What are the components of a will to create Brand Harmony?

The Will to Reallocate Resources

Are you willing to take money from your advertising budget and use it to train employees to Be the Brand? Are you willing to spend less money on generating leads through direct mail, and use the savings to put more people on the phones and improve the experience of the those people who respond to your offers?

Is your organization willing to shift a large share of its marketing staff's focus from external marketing to internal marketing? Are you willing to have marketing professionals who previously worked on glamorous advertising campaigns pay attention to the mundane details of how customers work their way through your voice mail system?

If an organization is going to make the transition from brute force branding to Brand Harmony, it will need to shift its allocation of marketing resources accordingly. Money and time that were once allocated to large-scale advertising and direct marketing campaigns will now need to be shared with efforts that reach customers at points throughout the customer life cycle. Marketing budgets are not entitlements that are automatically bequeathed to each year's successive generations of marketing programs. Your ad agency and brochure printer do not have an inalienable right to a guaranteed share of your budget, and you must be willing to disappoint people as you reallocate your funds.

In general, creating Brand Harmony is more people intensive than creating brute force branding. Marketing professionals faced this challenge before in the 1980's and early 1990's as organizations shifted advertising funds to more labor intensive direct marketing projects. The direct mail programs had many more components that the advertising programs, but most organizations didn't take this into account when staffing these projects, and people working on direct mail projects had to do a lot of scrambling.

'Head count' is a resource that organizations control as if it were weapons-grade uranium, only allowing access to it after the most acrobatic bureaucratic justifications. Successful creation of Brand Harmony requires that this taboo be broken, and organizations need to be willing to shift spending on inanimate objects, such as ads and brochures, into spending on the living, breathing human beings who will make Brand Harmony happen.

The Will to Have a Strong Executional Focus

Marketing programs based on Brand Harmony have many more 'moving parts' than traditional marketing programs based on advertising, direct marketing and promotion, for the simple reason that Brand Harmony recognizes all customer touch-points as marketing media.

Aligning all of these moving parts into a coherent, orchestrated set of experiences for customers won't happen automatically. Successfully creating Brand Harmony in the minds of your customers requires a focus on execution and implementation beyond what is normally required in marketing programs.

Many organizations will fail at creating Brand Harmony in their customers' minds because they won't be able to manage these moving parts. As mentioned in the previous point, the creation of Brand Harmony is more people intensive than brute force branding, and the focus of these people must be on *getting things done*. Brand Harmony requires an attention to detail that corresponds directly to the enhanced level of detail that customers are using to evaluate products. If you don't pay attention to ensuring that you are executing well at all points in the customer life cycle, your customer will certainly notice it, because she is paying attention to it.

The Will of Marketers to be Project Managers

In the last chapter we discussed how marketing people need to function less as orchestral soloists and more as orchestra conductors, coordinating and supporting the interactions that other people throughout the organization have with customers. In addition to being like conductors, marketers also have to be like project managers, taking responsibility for the execution and implementation that are so critical to the creation of Brand Harmony.

As resources are allocated to new activities, and the organization takes on a stronger executional focus in its marketing, marketing people need to take on the role of ensuring that it all happens. They need to have an ability to manage complex projects which involve departments throughout the organization. They are the primary orchestrators of Brand Harmony, seeing the details, monitoring the progress, making adjustments, keeping things on track. This is an important part of what marketing people do to Be the Brand.

This might not be a lot of fun for many marketing people, because it won't seem as creative as the marketing profession they originally entered. But that's only a matter of perspective. Blending Brand Harmony with a skill and sensitivity rivaling that of a musical composer or a chef can be a very creative activity. The marketing professionals who can see the beauty in creating Brand Harmony, and follow through by making it all happen, will be those with rewarding, enriching marketing careers in the future.

The Will for Senior Management to be Role Models

Most senior executives see marketing as something other people do.

In a world of Brand Harmony, however, senior executives are keenly involved in marketing. People throughout the organization are being asked to Be the Brand and consider themselves part of the marketing process, and these people will take their cues from the senior managers to whom they report. One of the most important ways senior managers can Be the Brand is to be a model for the organization's employees in everything they say and do.

A senior executive of a large company once told me that he felt like everything he said was like "whispering through a megaphone." The voice of a senior executive reverberates through an organization, whether the executive intends it to or not. The slightest hint that the guys at the top do not fully support the brand strategy can be the death knell for Brand Harmony.

Imagine a chain of clothing stores is implementing a program of Brand Harmony. Employees at all of the stores have eagerly embraced the challenge to Be the Brand, and the store managers are dutifully supporting the program in their locations. The divisional vice president supports the program, but at a regional meeting he makes a joke about one small part of it with which he disagrees. He doesn't think much of the comment, since he thinks he's 99% in agreement with the Brand Harmony program. How much do you think this one little comment can affect the way the store managers feel about the program?

A lot.

In most organizations, the voices of senior executives are amplified not just through megaphones but through PA systems worthy of a Rolling Stones concert. Everything thing they say, every move they make, every smirk or frown is interpreted, reinterpreted and reacted to. Senior executives need to turn this power toward the direction of supporting the brand strategy. They need to use the brand essence as the core concept in every communication they make inside the company.

For this reason, marketing people need to see senior executives as primary customers of their internal marketing program, with the goal of persuading these executives to play an active role—every day, every minute—in reinforcing the internal brand.

In this way, senior executives can play an important role in helping marketing people in their function as orchestra conductor. Marketing people are charged with persuading people in departments throughout the company to support the brand strategy and Be the Brand. It is not a foregone conclusion that everyone will cooperate—on the contrary, it is likely that many people outside of the marketing department will be pre-disposed not to listen to the direction of the marketing department. Senior executives with jurisdiction over those other departments can, through their signaling and support, make it much more likely that the entire organization can get in sync to deliver Brand Harmony.

Marketing is not a function that senior executives can delegate or ignore. In a world of Brand Harmony, it is a key part of their jobs ...not unlike everyone else in the organization.

The Will to Break Down the Boundaries Between Marketing and Operations

In a world of brute force branding, marketing people do marketing and operations people do operations. In a world of Brand Harmony, the lines between marketing and operations are blurred.

Operations people need to reorient their processes and mindset to recognize the role they play in motivating customer behavior. And marketing people, unlike the days when they could create advertising from an isolated cocoon, need to ensure that the Brand Harmony they wish to orchestrate is operationally feasible.

This intermingling of operations and marketing functions is fundamental to the creation of Brand Harmony. But it is a completely foreign concept to most organizations. Therefore, it is one reason many companies won't be able to create Brand Harmony.

Why is this so difficult?

The ingrained mindset of most marketing and operations people does not allow them to see where their functions overlap. Years of separately "doing their own thing" and carving out their own turf makes it difficult even to see the benefits of integration. Also, most have spent their entire careers in either marketing or operations jobs, but rarely in both. A look at the conflicts between marketing and operations in many organizations reveals how little these areas even understand what the others do.

Operations and marketing departments are often located at distant points on the organization chart from each other, like distant cousins on a family tree. Each area has its own culture of self-preservation, and its own system for maintaining its way of life. As mentioned above, operations people are not predisposed to taking direction from the marketing department, and marketing people are often not interested in constraining their creativity with operational realities. There are many managerial biases that stand in the way of integrating the way marketing and operations disciplines serve customers.

Despite how challenging this is, organizations need to figure it out. They have no choice. If organizations are myopic and unable to see clear to a way to integrate operations and marketing under a common Brand Harmony strategy, their customers will see the non-sense of this with an acute clarity.

This is a very good example of the important role that senior executives play. Brand Harmony favors CEO's and other senior executives who recognize that marketing and operations aren't discrete dukedoms, but interdependent functions between which customers don't distinguish. Any executive who, in his or her lofty position at the "top" of the organization chart, has common responsibility for both marketing and operations can play a critical role in breaking down these barriers and improving the organization's chances for creating Brand Harmony.

The Will to Stay the Course

Much of the marketing that companies do falls into campaigns or finite projects. For example, advertising happens in campaigns or flights that are refreshed periodically. Direct mail is often grouped into discrete initiatives. Promotions are seasonally based or are planned to address particular business situations, such as the roll-out of a new product or under-performing sales volume.

The creation of Brand Harmony doesn't work like this. Brand Harmony recognizes that brand impressions are built cumulatively over time, and customers won't 'get it' if messages change with the seasons. The evolution of Brand Harmony needs to make sense as time unfolds, just as the story told in a song must make sense as it develops over time.

Moreover, Brand Harmony requires people throughout the organization, sometimes numbering in the thousands, to deliver complementary messages to customers. Getting everyone in the organization to understand the message in the first place will be hard enough; changing it on them as frequently as ad campaigns are changed will create mass confusion.

So, unlike brute force branding, Brand Harmony requires an organization to see its marketing projects as being part of an ongoing process that evolves over time. Instead of looking at marketing as a series of campaigns, Brand Harmony looks at marketing programs and projects as critical pieces of the continuous fabric of the organization's ongoing operations.

An organization successfully creating Brand Harmony has core, stable business processes that enable it to deliver its brand promise continuously. Employees know what it takes for them to Be the Brand, and this knowledge has been with them long enough that they have substantial experience actually being the brand. Marketing programs and projects all reinforce and develop these core processes. They are not invented ad hoc, but are developed out of this ongoing process.

The kind of patience and commitment this approach requires is a challenge for leaders in many organizations. Sticking with a game plan can be a little boring, especially for executives whose careers have been defined by reacting defensively to a series of crises and 'fires' that crop up throughout their day. Many senior executives look at the business world as a series of disconnected transactions and discrete events, making it difficult to stick with core strategies for long periods of time. Most of them did not accomplish their rise to the top by "staying the course," but by moving nimbly from project to project, swashbuckling their way to success. They are easily bored, and are very eager to move on to the next pressing challenge that is filling their voice mail and email in-boxes.

Brand harmony won't let anyone get away with this. Brand Harmony isn't like a trip to the dentist—something you do a few times a year, and only more frequently in the face of an acute problem. It's much more like breathing, something you never stop doing. Brand impressions are fleeting, unstable thoughts in customers' minds, and they can be damaged as soon as the customer encounters a dissonant expression of the product. Brand Harmony gets no days off.

Most companies can write a long list of obituaries for programs that died before their time. Some programs deserved to be terminated, but in many cases they died more from corporate boredom and a short attention span than for any good business reason. Too many companies take a "launch and leave" attitude that dooms young programs to failure before they have a chance to develop into something valuable.

Overcoming corporate boredom is critical to the creation of Brand Harmony. Marketing strategies should not be changed because the calendar says it's time, or because of a senior manager's whim. These strategies should evolve from a thorough, company-wide understanding of the relationship between the customers and the business. When it comes to Brand Harmony, patience is definitely a virtue.

To help you stay the course, make it clear to employees throughout your organization that it is not only safe, but encouraged to speak up if they see the company take a wrong turn on the road to Brand Harmony. Employees in organizations can usually see very clearly when their companies stray off course, but most will sit passively and not say anything without this kind of encouragement. On a recent business trip to Minneapolis I rented a car with a GPS unit. Despite the navigation help, I missed an exit. Suddenly I heard a voice saying, "Recalculating route." Think of the value of having a navigation system for your Brand Harmony program that will alert you of wrong turns before it's too late! Make sure that people throughout your organization feel comfortable setting off alarm bells if your Brand Harmony efforts start to lose direction.

Conclusion

Marketing's Copernican Revolution

Imagine yourself in a rented public meeting hall in Lancaster, California, the home of the Flat Earth Society. The linoleum floor is cracked, the fluorescent lights are a bit harsh, the smell of Salisbury Steak wafts in through the kitchen's swinging doors. Charles Johnson, president of the Flat Earth Society is at the podium:

> "One thing we know for sure about this world...the known inhabited world is Flat, Level, a Plain World. The Fact the Earth is Flat is not my opinion, it is a Proved Fact. Also demonstrated (sic) Sun and Moon are about 3,000 miles away are both 32 miles across. The Planets are 'tiny.' Sun and Moon do Move, earth does NOT move, whirl, spin or gyrate."[11]

The room erupts in applause. You are confused. Why is everyone so enamored with a world view that is so out of date? Mr. Johnson continues:

"If Earth were a ball spinning in space, there would be no up or down. Australians do NOT hang by their feet under the world...this is a FACT, not a theory!"[12]

You sit there stunned and think to yourself: "You can see the world the old way, or you can see it the new way."

In spite of what Mr. Johnson and his Flat Earth Society followers perceive to be the truth, there is too much contradictory evidence to support their point of view. The revelations of Copernicus and Galileo, followed by three hundred years of subsequent scientific discovery, have rendered Mr. Johnson's views defunct.

Similarly, if we are willing to look at the natural laws that govern branding, it's not hard to see evidence that the idea of brute force branding is as obsolete as the idea of a flat earth. In a marketplace driven by powerful customers, it takes a lot more than brute force to create brand impressions. Yet, most marketing discussions have, at their core, a perspective that is based on big companies sending out big messages through big advertising campaigns.

The way much marketing and branding are practiced today reminds me of the way the Flat Earth Society looks at the world—people choosing to ignore the evidence presented by the world around them and stubbornly hanging on to old views about how the things work.

Marketing needs to go through a revolution of thought that abandons these Flat Earth marketing ideas and works from a set of principles that are more realistic in a world of intense customer power. It is, on a smaller scale, reminiscent of the revolution wrought by the thinking of visionaries like Copernicus and Galileo, who, under great peril, proposed a new view of the universe based on fresh observation of the physical world.

Before Copernicus, our common belief was that the earth was at the center of the universe, with the sun and other celestial bodies revolving around it. We saw ourselves as the crown of creation, and it only made sense that we would be at the epicenter of the universe, as the all-important focal point of everything that existed.

However, by the 2nd century it started to become clear that the physical reality we observed in the sky didn't conform to our idea of a geocentric universe. For the next 1,400 years we resisted the obvious, creating convoluted explanations for elliptical orbits and other observed phenomena which contradicted our beliefs. We hung on to our world view like a cherished security blanket, and it wasn't until Copernicus, and then Galileo, that we were able to forget what we "knew," and accept a more plausible explanation of reality. At the center of this new perspective was the realization that the universe is much bigger than us, and that we are relatively inconsequential.

Marketing is approaching its Copernican moment. Up until now, marketers have seen themselves at the center of the branding universe. To these marketers, a brand exists because a marketer has decided it should exist. Like the sun, moon and stars orbiting the earth, this marketing-centric view sees everything else about the brand—its delivery, the underlying product and even its customers—as consequences, per se, of the brand, which exist only to pay homage to it.

Smart marketers now recognize that they are no longer at the center of the branding universe. As customer power increases, the physics of branding become harder to ignore. It has become clear that it is the customer, not the marketer, who defines the brand for himself, in his own mind. And, it is also clear that a brand isn't what the marketer says it is but what the customer thinks it is.

Sigmund Freud said that the common element of all scientific revolutions is that we learn that we are not as important as we previously thought. In addition to the Copernican discovery that the earth is not the center of the universe, Freud adds two more examples: Darwin's insight that man is not the central life form on earth and his own discovery that man is not even in total control of his own mind, i.e. that there are unconscious processes that determine our actions without our awareness. Brand Harmony follows this pattern, taking marketers off their pedestal at the center of brand creation, assigning them a more supportive, coordinating role around its edges.

This is going to be hard for many people, in marketing and all other disciplines of business. The Flat Earth mentality I've described ignores evidence from the world around us, blinded by the advertising-driven status quo in the same way the critics of Copernicus and Galileo couldn't see reality through the fog of dogma.

Marketing's Copernican Revolution will be a humbling one because it will show marketers that it is not them, but customers, who are at the center of the branding universe. But this humility can be liberating. A heretic once chided a religious man, saying that Copernicus proved that man, supposedly created in God's image, is a small, inconsequential being in a vast universe. "Yes," the religious man responded, "but man is a fabulous astronomer."

Maybe our new humbling perspective, in the wake of marketing's Copernican revolution, will help us be better astronomers, seeing the branding universe from our customers' perspectives, helping us to hear the harmony of the spheres in the same way that our customers hear it as they experience our products.

Appendix

What to Do When You Finish Reading this Book:
*Create a Grassroots Brand Harmony Revolution
in Your Company!*

Brand Harmony is inherently a communal concept. Your customers
are paying attention to *everything* your company does, so Brand
Harmony will only work if people from throughout your entire organization collaborate to orchestrate your customer's total experience.

The implementation steps in this book are designed for groups
of people in an organization to work through together. If you're
the boss, encourage your people to get together and do these
implementation steps. If you're not the boss, don't wait for per-
mission! Get a group of colleagues together and get started!

Here are suggestions for doing the implementation steps:

• Identify 3–6 colleagues who work with you to form your core
  team and be your partners in this process. (If you work by yourself, enlist the help of people who know you well and understand
  what you do.) Select people with different perspectives, but make
  sure to assemble a group of people who trust each other. You
  want to encourage debate and differences of opinion, and it's
  important that the conversation can be open and constructive.
  See www.brandharmony.com/invite, where you'll be able to send
  these colleagues information about Brand Harmony and how it
  can help your organization.

- Have your team members read this book. It won't take them long; after a few hours of reading, you should all have a shared understanding of the principles of Brand Harmony. Form a Brand Harmony reading group, meeting at lunch or over coffee to review chapters, work through the implementation steps, and discuss how to make Brand Harmony work for your organization. See www.brandharmony.com/reading-group for ideas and information.

- Do the implementation steps one at a time. You'll be able to gauge when you're ready to move on to the next implementation step. Be sure to look ahead so you can do any preparation in plenty of time.

- For the brainstorming portion of each implementation step, gather the group into a room and commit to uninterrupted time to complete the step. Take notes on easel paper, papering the walls of the room with the sheets as you move through the implementation steps.[13] Putting your ideas and insights up on the wall makes it easier for everyone in the meeting to absorb the information and interact with each other.

- As you move through the implementation steps, it will help to go back and review the relevant sections of the text that relate to each step as you do them.

- Be free thinking...avoid comments like, *"Oh, we'll never fix that, so let's ignore it,"* or, *"We can't talk about that problem because everybody knows it's the boss's son-in-law's fault."* Lift yourselves above the internal biases and constraints of your organization; be honest with yourselves, but always have an optimistic look toward *'what could be.'*

- When you're done with each brainstorming session, consolidate the notes from the easel paper into text on your computer, organizing and filtering the information so that you end up with a workable, accessible set of insights from each of the implementation steps.

- Broaden your circle! As you move through the implementation steps, begin inviting more people to your sessions.

- Spread the word! Start telling people throughout the organization about the insights you're gathering. Start looking for people whose actions have an important effect on customer experiences and on people who have the ability to influence others throughout the organization to buy into the idea of Brand Harmony. Don't just focus on "assigned leaders", i.e., senior people with lofty titles. Sure, they count...a lot! But there are probably many people with "earned leadership" in your company who can influence others purely by the power of their performance, insights and personality.

- As you're trying to sell this process to your colleagues, whether it is people you work with, people you work for or people who work for you, be sure to use the principles of Brand Harmony. Make sure that everything they hear or see about your Brand Harmony initiative helps them understand why it is important. Orchestrate all of their interactions with you and your team in a way that makes them say, "I get it! We have to do this! And I want to be part of it!"

- Get formal backing for the process. As you begin to find compelling, tangible opportunities to improve your customers' experience of Brand Harmony, get the organization to recognize your "movement" as a legitimate strategic process.

- Stick with it! That may be the most important piece of advice in this book.

Be sure to share your success stories with us! Just email us at successstories@brandharmony.com.

Endnotes

1 http://www.homesashore.com/Advertising/advertising.html

2 http://www.thinking.net/Systems_Thinking/ST_Fallacies/
st_fallacies.html

3 Ibid.

4 At a McDonald's owner/operator convention years ago that
coincided with the opening of McDonald's 10,000th restaurant, a manager asked then-chairman Fred Turner when
McDonald's was going to diversify into other businesses. "We
now have 20,000 bathrooms," Turner responded. "Let me
know when they're all clean, and then we'll talk about getting
into other businesses."

5 *New York Times Magazine,* April 30, 2000

6 I heard this story in a speech Jerry Hirschberg gave at the
Equity Office National Conference, April 30, 2001.

7 *New York Time Magazine,* December 1, 2002, page 96

8 An example of different brand strategies for different groups
comes from my time as vice-president of resort marketing for
Hyatt Hotels: Our resort hotels served both vacationers and
planners of group business meetings. These two groups clearly needed to think about our resorts in different ways. Same
product, different (but related) desired brand perceptions.

9   Stephen Palmquist, *The Tree of Philosophy: A course of introductory lectures for beginning students of philosophy,* 4th Edition, (Hong Kong, Philosophy Press, 2000), p. 16.

10 I would like to acknowledge Jared Diamond for this metaphor, who described "The Anna Karenina Principle" in his book *Guns, Germs and Steel* (W.W. Norton & Co., 1999) to illustrate why most animals were not suitable candidates for human domestication. A single problem, such as the tendency to panic, a slow growth rate or a carnivorous diet, is enough to make an animal unsuitable for domestication, even if the species met every other criterion. Diamond writes, "We tend to seek easy, single-factor explanations of success. For most things, though, success actually requires avoiding many separate possible causes of failure." (p. 157)

11 Charles Johnson was president of the Flat Earth Society until his death in March, 2001. The quotes are taken verbatim from a flyer published by the Flat Earth Society and from a 1984 *Newsweek* interview with Mr. Johnson. The Flat Earth Society is located at PO Box 2533, Lancaster, CA, 93539, telephone 805/727-1635. Yep, they really exist.

12 Ibid.

13 I recommend 3M Post-it self-adhesive easel paper and a bunch of colored markers for this process. I like the 3M Post-it easel paper because you can attach it and reattach it to the walls multiple times as you complete the implementation steps and review the notes from your sessions. Trying to do that with tape is a mess.

Glossary

Explanation of terms and phrases used in this book.

Anna Karenina Principle: The first line of Tolstoy's masterpiece *Anna Karenina* is *"All happy families are alike; every unhappy family is unhappy in its own way."* The same thing happens to companies. All companies who work in sync to create Brand Harmony are comprised of teams of people who work together well and follow a common strategy, seeing their entire organization as one large "marketing department." But, each company who fails at Brand Harmony does so in its own unique way, finding some special way of translating its own internal conflict into a one-of-a-kind way of confusing and disinteresting customers. (See page 133 and endnote #9)

'Be the Brand': When employees understand the personal role they each play in contributing to customers' perceptions of Brand Harmony, and act in a way that supports that role.

Bigger isn't Better: The phenomenon in which the competitive advantage in branding has shifted from favoring large companies with large marketing budgets to smaller companies who can more easily get their entire organization *in sync* to create Brand Harmony.

Brand: What a customer thinks about a product. Your brand is not what you say you are, but what your customer thinks you are.

Brand Awareness: A measure of how many people know about a product. Frequently misinterpreted as the best measure of a brand's strength, brand awareness is the most overrated branding metric.

Brand Consonance: When a customer perceives that a product's experiences blend together, but they don't say anything compelling. Brand consonance is a weak form of Brand Harmony.

Brand Dissonance: When a customer perceives that a product's experiences are in conflict. Brand dissonance discourages a customer from being more involved with a product.

Brand Entropy: Entropy is one of the most powerful forces in the universe, causing systems to move progressively from states of organization to states of more disorganization and diffusion. Without a strong brand essence to act as a glue, *brand entropy* will take over, your organization will act in a more disintegrated fashion, and the experiences customers have with your product will become less complementary and more dissonant.

Brand Essence: The shared soul of your brand, the spark of which is present in every experience a customer has with your product. The "DNA" of your brand.

Brand Harmony: The idea that the strength of a customer's brand impression is driven not by how many times the customer sees your ad, or by how clever that ad is, but by how well all experiences this customer has with your product blend to tell a sensible, cumulative story.

Brand Impression: A customer's cumulative thought or opinion of a product.

Brand Irrelevance: When a customer perceives (or, for that matter, fails to notice) that various experiences with a product do not reinforce each other.

Brute Force Branding: The most prevalent approach to branding over the last 50 years, in which strong brand impressions are believed to be created by repeated exposure to strong messages.

Business Objectives: The goals of all marketing efforts.

Cognitive Dissonance: A theory developed by Leon Festinger in the 1950's to describe how humans have an innate need to reduce the perception of conflict between different thoughts or concepts.

Customer: Any person whose behavior affects the results of your product. (Think about it—this means a vendor could actually be a customer.)

Customer Power: The irreversible, tectonic shift in power from people who sell things to people who buy things. The most powerful change in the world of marketing over the last 50 years.

Customer Touch-point: Any point of contact between a customer and a product. Product experiences occur at customer touch-points.

Customer Touch-point Mapping: Identifying all of the points of contact between your customers and your product throughout the life cycle of those customers' relationships with your organization.

Desired Brand Perception: What you would like people to think about your product. Successful implementation of Brand Harmony narrows the gap between your desired brand perception and your customer's actual brand perception.

Fully Integrated Marketing: Marketing that considers each and every possible interaction a customer has with a product to be an important marketing communication.

Internal Marketing: Orchestrating the experiences employees have with an organization in a way that encourages them to Be the Brand and say with enthusiasm and commitment, "I get it. I know what I am supposed to do to contribute to the Brand Harmony we are trying to create."

Life Cycle Marketing: Brand Harmony is built over time throughout the *life cycle* of a customer's relationship with your organization. *Life cycle marketing* is the continual orchestration of customer experiences as this relationship grows, helping the customer better understand your brand promise while getting to know you better.

Marketing: Any activities that work to persuade customers to behave in a way that improves a product's performance. Good marketing actually encourages customers to behave in a way that improves product performance. Bad marketing discourages customers from behaving in that way.

Marketing's Copernican Revolution: The epic change that demonstrates to marketers that they are no longer at the center of the marketing universe, but have been replaced there by their customers.

Mistaken Completeness: The frequently occurring phenomenon in which people believe that they have a larger portion of the available information about a subject than they actually have. When this happens, people commonly extrapolate from that limited and incomplete information to what they believe is a comprehensive understanding of that subject.

Myths: Shared perspectives and beliefs of a community. A myth may or may not be true, but its believers don't even think to ask that question; they just believe. A strong myth within a company's culture can influence the way employees interact with customers, for better or for worse.

Panning for Gold: The process of exploring a vast array of business issues in an open-minded way that allows the most important issues to shine and stand out, shouting, "Hey, I'm really important."

Personalization: Orchestrating the product experiences of an individual customer in a way that encourages that customer to perceive a Brand Harmony that is most personally relevant and motivating to him or her.

Picture of Success: A clear, detailed description of the business outcomes an organization aims for.

Product: Any offering that a customer could acquire a benefit from. Whenever the word "product" is used in this book, it could mean a physical product or any kind of service offering.

Product Experience: Any interaction a customer has with a product or service, including not only direct encounters with the product itself, but also any communications about the product, interactions with people who represent the product, hearsay or word of mouth about the product, etc. In other words, any experience that can influence the customer's opinion of the product is a product experience.

Tabasco Sauce Effect: How a small but powerful product experience can affect a customer's overall sense of Brand Harmony. A little can go a long way.

Unique Selling Proposition: An antiquated, anachronistic term that marketers use to describe what sets their product apart. Now replaced with the more customer-focused term "desired brand perception."

Walgreen's Seven Service Basics: Sorry. I still haven't found someone who can tell me. (See page 125)